PRINCETON STUDIES IN INTERNATIONAL

The External Liquidity of an Advanced Country

Weir M. Brown

INTERNATIONAL FINANCE SECTION

DEPARTMENT OF ECONOMICS

PRINCETON UNIVERSITY · 1964

This is the fourteenth number in the series PRINCE-TON STUDIES IN INTERNATIONAL FINANCE, published from time to time under the sponsorship of the International Finance Section of the Department of Economics at Princeton University.

The author, Weir M. Brown, is Deputy Chief of the U.S. Delegation to the Organization for Economic Cooperation and Development, Paris, and U.S. Treasury Representative. This paper represents the personal views of the author and should not be interpreted as constituting the opinions of any institution or governmental agency.

This series is intended to be restricted to meritorious research studies in the general field of international financial problems, both policy and theory, which are too long for the journals and too short to warrant publication as books. The Section welcomes the submission of manuscripts for this series.

While the Section sponsors the STUDIES, the writers are free to develop their topics as they will. Their ideas and treatment may or may not be shared by the editorial committee of the Section or the members of the Department.

FRITZ MACHLUP
Director

Princeton University

PRINCETON STUDIES IN INTERNATIONAL FINANCE NO. 14

The External Liquidity of an Advanced Country

Weir M. Brown

INTERNATIONAL FINANCE SECTION
DEPARTMENT OF ECONOMICS
PRINCETON UNIVERSITY · 1964

Printed in the United States of America by Princeton University Press,

at Princeton, New Jersey

TABLE OF CONTENTS

STATISTICAL ANNEX

I. *Country Tables and Charts*

II. *Summary Tables—Group of Ten Countries*

THE EXTERNAL LIQUIDITY OF AN ADVANCED COUNTRY*

I. INTRODUCTION

The term liquidity is gradually taking on a somewhat more precise and commonly accepted meaning. At the beginning, as so often happens in economic discussion, references to "the liquidity problem" were picked up, like a piece of shiny quartz, by us savages in government service or the press and brandished or carried around with us as a talisman until the wiser men in the village began to examine the shiny concept to identify its content and determine whether it could take on a fine cutting edge. Through careful analysis, considerable progress already has been made in defining a meaningful concept of liquidity, comparing it with the somewhat narrower but likewise slippery concept of reserves, and separating liquidity itself from the question of whether its availability is adequate or in shortage. Regarding the latter point, it is becoming increasingly understood that the relationship between a country's liquidity position and other economic variables, and the manner in which this relationship may change over time, are more complex than at first presumed. Analysis of these latter questions, as well as the more heated discussion of various prescribed remedies for putative deficiencies in liquidity, is of course being intensively pursued.

In the present article, with the aid of the now more clearly articulated concept of external liquidity, the pertinent relationships to other financial phenomena are further explored with the hope of adding to the understanding of these functional relationships and their policy implications. In method, the exposition will be primarily theoretical. It will, however, be illustrated by reference from time to time to statistical material assembled in the Annex. The statistics tabulated there relate to the countries known as the Group of Ten[1] and are

* The author wishes to acknowledge his appreciation to the Secretariat of the Organization for Economic Cooperation and Development (O.E.C.D.), and especially to M. Raoul Gross of its Economics and Statistics Department, for making available and advising on the use of balance-of-payments data. M. Serge R. Foy assisted the author very effectively in preparing the tables and charts.

[1] More precisely, the series cover the ten I.M.F. member countries which entered into the Special Borrowing Arrangement with the Fund (Belgium, Canada, France, Germany, Italy, Japan, Netherlands, Sweden, United Kingdom, and United States) plus Switzerland. See International Monetary Fund, *Summary Proceedings, Annual Meeting, 1962*, p. 19.

shown separately by country. Apart from the simplification gained by such a selection, there are good reasons for concentrating the analysis on this group of countries whose currencies are internationally significant; not only do they dispose over 70 percent of total liquidity resources, but their institutional arrangements are relatively homogeneous, and they occupy a dominant policy position with respect to monetary affairs. Still more pertinently, it is precisely the non-reserve-currency countries of this group of advanced nations about which the apprehension has been commonly expressed that their liquidity position will become progressively less adequate. Analysis of that hypothesis of increasing inadequacy will occupy a major place in this paper.

II. DEFINITIONS OF LIQUIDITY

As a definition for the term external liquidity used in this article, the definition developed by Wood in his excellent paper seems acceptable. The external liquidity of a country is defined as "such resources as are readily available to its monetary authorities for the purpose of financing temporary deficits in its balance of payments and defending the stability of its rate of exchange."[2]

This definition is acceptable and usable. It has the virtue of stating as explicitly as possible the principal shades of connotation ordinarily implied when the term liquidity is employed in current usage. While being acceptable, it is far from ideal, and the trouble with the definition is as much with the subject term itself as with the predicate. As used in current monetary discussion and as defined above, the term refers to the means-of-international-payment held by and accessible to a country's monetary authorities. One could wish that some term more accurate descriptively and functionally, such as "reserve availability," might have been chosen. That might, for instance, have reduced some of the sources of ambiguity about whether liquidity refers to a quantity (which is how it is ordinarily employed in this paper), or a quality, or an absolute or relative capacity.[3] But the red men encountered by Columbus in Central America have become for all time

[2] Ralph C. Wood, "Conceptual Aspects of International Liquidity" (unpublished paper, September 1963), p. 5. See also J. Marcus Fleming, "International Liquidity: Ends and Means," I.M.F. *Staff Papers*, Vol. III, No. 3 (December 1961), p. 439.
[3] See the careful analysis on this point by Fritz Machlup, "Liquidité Nationale et Internationale," Banque Nationale de Belgique, *Bulletin d'Information et de Documentation* (February 1962).

"Indians," and we do not need to insist on renaming external "liquidity."

As in every other field of orderly discussion, any term can be adopted so long as there is an accepted understanding as to what phenomena, processes, etc., it embraces. The definition of external liquidity adopted above has the merit of incorporating the essential characteristics of the resources themselves and of relating them functionally to given purposes, the whole matter being viewed from the standpoint of the monetary authorities of the country in question. (Since the orientation is that of a single country, the term "external liquidity" seems preferable to "international liquidity," although some authors—including Wood—use the two interchangeably.)

At several significant places in the definition there is seen to be a word or phrase of considerable elasticity of meaning or measurement. It is perfectly apparent, for example, that such terms as "readily available" take on a wider or narrower meaning according to circumstances. Do we mean resources which are conditionally accessible to the authorities, as well as those without conditions; to what extent are commercial banks' foreign assets considered as "available," etc.? These possibilities of variation in concept and measurement have been explored exhaustively by others,[4] with the general result that such elastic elements in the definition are not a weakness but, on the contrary, offer a certain resiliency which is useful.

In the statistical data presented in the Annex for the key countries, the easy adaptability and mental correction which can be indulged in the pure definition-making stage are not sufficient, and it is necessary to encounter the concrete problem of making measurement choices among available time series, without knowing in which past recorded year or which unknown future year a more expanded or contracted measure of "readily available" financial resources than the one chosen may give a more precise idea of the liquidity position of the country.

The definition of liquidity has been described above as possessing, at several points, degrees of flexibility which permit it to be adapted according to circumstances. Nevertheless, for the purposes of the present analysis it has seemed desirable to decide which degree of width or narrowness of definition provides the most meaningful measure for general purposes. The author has been guided by the fact

[4] See especially the articles by Wood and Machlup cited above, as well as the present author's "The Concept and Measurement of Foreign Exchange Reserves," *Economic Journal* (September 1955).

that the concept of external liquidity grows by extension out of the more established idea of monetary reserves, and that the difference between them lies primarily in the extent to which the notion of liquidity embraces resources not held by the monetary authorities of the given country but available to them.

Before leaving this examination of the definition of liquidity for a consideration of some of its applications, it may be pertinent to annotate the main "flexible points" of the liquidity definition so as to indicate what are the most likely choices for general application. The areas of choice will be discussed under three main headings: gross versus net resources; conditional versus unconditional availability; and public versus public-plus-private resources. Often the decision made under one of these headings tends to influence and be influenced by the other headings.

1. *Gross versus net resources.* Whether to consider the external resources available to the country's monetary authorities on a gross basis or to offset its external liabilities is a familiar and anguished question that has been well explored in the literature on external reserves. The main conclusion there reached—i.e., that neither treatment is correct or incorrect and that either or both may need to be applied in some circumstances—is also valid when extended to the broader field of liquidity. For most purposes, however, it seems somewhat preferable to deal mainly with gross resources. This is only in part because net resources present greater conceptual problems when they are aggregated for many countries. Several advantages of the gross measurement remain even when no summation of countries is intended. When a country goes into balance-of-payments deficit or finds its currency under pressure for other reasons, it is difficult to predict whether the central bank will be confronted with calls to liquidate its liabilities to foreign holders (usually official institutions), thus reducing the adequacy of its gross assets vis-à-vis the overall external balance, and, if so, at what stage in the disequilibrium. Secondly, as a practical matter, among the Group of Ten countries liabilities to other central banks have not been quantitatively large except in the United States and the United Kingdom (although this has altered somewhat as a result of the adoption of reciprocal currency swap arrangements).

A most important argument in favor of working with gross rather than net resources is that, whatever may be the desirability on suitable occasions of considering a country's net position in direct reserve holdings, when we have moved from the concept of reserve holdings to the extended concept of liquidity, which includes credits externally accessible, the idea of measuring net resources potentially available to and from the country becomes even less feasible than before.

2. *Conditional versus unconditional availability.* This paper tends to include as additional external resources only those which are relatively certainly available, without extraordinary conditions. This could well include, in addition to the "owned reserves" in gold and convertible currencies, such assets or availabilities as currencies available for drawing under stand-by arrangements, the I.M.F. gold and first credit tranche, and foreign loans callable on unilateral demand. It would not include, for example, special credits to be negotiated or loans owed by a foreign government but subject to a fixed amortization schedule. (The data used in this paper for purposes of the standard tables are described in Section IV below.)

3. *Are private resources included?* From a theoretical standpoint, it would usually be correct to consider the present and potential foreign resources of the commercial banks as additive to those of the central monetary authorities, and, under the convention adopted above, these would likewise be considered on a gross basis. Such holdings of foreign currencies can be sold to domestic firms to pay for imports; and when the local currency is under strain the central bank often can, by monetary measures, entice the repatriation of some commercial banks' balances, thus adding to its own holdings. Yet that is sometimes possible only at the cost of either overly drastic credit contraction at home or by forcing repatriation through foreign-exchange control. Assets so obtained by the monetary authorities would violate both (a) our disposition to disregard resources which are only conditionally available and (b) our basic general decision to study the liquidity problem with special reference to advanced countries maintaining a high degree of convertibility.

There are other obstacles to the inclusion of privately held foreign-currency assets. One secondary reason, from the standpoint of measurement, is that for some countries the commercial-bank data are only available on a net basis, whereas it seems preferable to measure official holdings grossly. Moreover, even when the gross assets and liabilities of the commercial banks are shown separately, for some countries the data give the net "foreign position" of assets in the domestic currency and foreign currencies combined. While it may be probable that the figures shown under "assets in foreign and domestic currencies," which have risen perceptibly in the past five years, rep-

5

resent predominantly foreign-currency assets, for any individual country this is not necessarily the case. Another consideration of major theoretical importance is that even if we could obtain reliable and comparable figures on the gross amounts of foreign currencies actually held by the commercial banks, there is no readily acceptable statistical or conceptual way of measuring how much would be available to them additionally through foreign credits. (It seems obvious that the Crédit Lyonnais has an availability of foreign credit beyond its present holdings of foreign currencies; but the amount of such additional resources for the French commercial banks is less determinate than the amounts available to the Banque de France at the I.M.F.)

To summarize these definitional notes: in addition to the gross foreign-currency resources presently held and potentially available abroad to the monetary authorities on a relatively unconditional basis, there are, according to circumstances, varying further amounts which are largely indeterminate and not subject to easy generalization but which could be made available conditionally, either from the commercial banks or through resort to foreign and international institutions. A country's liquidity is made up principally of two major components, both of which we have chosen to regard on a gross basis—those foreign-currency assets already held by the monetary authority and those financial resources available to it abroad on credit terms. With all due regard for the circumstances in which some other interpretation may become preferable or more pertinent, the writer employs in this paper an interpretation of external liquidity which tends to concentrate on a country's gross rather than net resources; on those secondary or borrowed resources available with very few conditions if any; and on *public* holdings and availabilities, largely to the exclusion of private resources.

III. ADEQUACY OF LIQUIDITY: A FIRST CONSIDERATION

Having established what is comprehended by the term external liquidity, the discussion can now proceed to the question of whether this liquidity is adequate or whether it is, or will become, in some sense "inadequate," as is sometimes declared. Formulation of the question obviously implies comparison of the amount of liquidity with some magnitude representing "requirements." Since the approach to be used will continue to be a general one, we shall be concerned less with specifying any present amounts or making detailed statistical projections than with examining the nature of the criteria suitable for determining adequacy or inadequacy of a country's liquidity.

It must be recalled that the definition adopted concerns liquidity from the viewpoint of the individual country. What is meaningful in any examination of the question of adequacy of liquidity, therefore, is to consider the volume of a country's liquidity against the functional needs or requirements which it is intended to serve. Throughout, attention is concentrated primarily upon the industrialized, financially important countries, and, in the present section, upon those countries other than the two reserve-currency countries.

What are the needs which establish the requirement of an advanced (non-reserve-currency) country for liquidity? How is this requirement determined by or related to significant magnitudes in the country's situation (GNP, volume of money, major balance-of-payments components, etc.), and how can this relation be expected to change? Studies on the subject of liquidity have usually dealt with this question of adequacy by comparing the amount of liquidity with the value of imports. To be more precise, the comparisons in fact have ordinarily been made between official reserves—rather than liquidity—and imports.[5] This form of presentation understates the volume of liquidity by ignoring the credit component, a component which has increased at irregular intervals in recent years as an absolute, and sometimes relative, portion of a country's total liquidity. Nevertheless, at this point, we are not concerned with the fact that liquidity had been only partially measured but with whether a country's import value constitutes a satisfactory indication of its requirement for liquidity.

The ratio of liquidity to imports is subject to many faults either as an explanation *ex post* of a given liquidity change or as a criterion for use by central banks in their "liquidity policy." Let us start with the latter, with the liquidity/import ratio as a prospective measure of monetary-resource requirements. Recent authors have pointed to the fact that in most countries there is no longer a close link, either by statute or by monetary policy, between the amount of monetary gold held by a country and the major macroeconomic variables of its domestic economy (price levels, money supply). They have passed from this observation, which was also valid to a large extent under the full gold standard, to the conclusion that a country's liquidity position

[5] See International Monetary Fund, *International Reserves and Liquidity* (Washington, 1958); Robert Triffin, *Gold and the Dollar Crisis* (New Haven: Yale University Press, 1960), especially Chapter 5.

is relevant only to its external requirements, which in turn they have measured in comparison with the value of imports. A country's reserves have been expressed as X per cent of its annual imports or as Y months of imports. Such a ratio implicitly assumes a situation in which the country would have no foreign-exchange receipts whatsoever and would face the necessity of covering its current (prosperity) level of imports entirely by liquidating its reserve holdings. Strictly speaking, it is only in this sense that a country's liquidity is equal to "Y months of imports."

This measurement is, on the one hand, not sufficiently rigorous, for other foreign expenditures besides those for merchandise imports would have to be financed. On the other hand, the standard is too rigorous, for a country is never entirely devoid of receipts even in the most extreme balance-of-payments crisis. The ratio reserves-to-imports might be applicable to a medieval walled city in a state of complete siege but is hardly appropriate to the situation of modern advanced economies, and it can be doubted that even Continental central bankers conceive of their contingencies in exactly these terms of complete physical siege.

What is much more relevant in a calculation of the adequacy of liquidity than the reserves-to-imports ratio is a comparison between liquidity and the country's net external balance, somehow defined. That is to say, the amount which the monetary authorities may be called upon to finance out of the gold and foreign currencies which they now hold or could readily obtain is the amount represented by a present or expected net imbalance in the country's balance of international payments. It is this that the monetary authorities will have in mind in pursuing their liquidity policy (apart from any reasons of internal economic policy that may occasionally dictate a change in reserve level). The respective payments for merchandise imports, services, and private and public capital transactions, on the one hand, and the corresponding receipts for these "above-the-line" items, on the other, will produce a balance which will have to be financed, in the balance-of-payments sense, and which probably will affect the liquidity position (up or down) of the monetary authorities.[6] It is not necessary to belabor the fact that a country's balance-of-payments position is a more meaningful measure against which to compare its liquidity than

[6] The fact that balance-of-payments presentations ordinarily show changes during the reporting period in the country's net position, whereas our preference is to measure liquidity in gross terms, does not alter the principle under discussion.

is its import volume. A country's imports may be rising steadily over a period of years, but the influence of that rise upon the country's current level of liquidity or its future liquidity requirements depends also upon what developments take place in other components of the balance of payments. An upward movement of imports, by itself, does not necessarily produce a corresponding increase in the country's requirements for liquidity.

Abandonment of the term imports in the adequacy ratio and its replacement by the net external balance is a change which appears both desirable and comforting. This is, first, because it constitutes a more logical indication of the external financing requirements which the monetary authority must contemplate, as stated above. Secondly, the net external balance, being a substantially smaller figure than imports, represents a much lower "requirement," and its use raises the apparent adequacy of a country's liquidity. Among the Group of Ten countries, the net external balance in foreign payments in recent years has, though considered large, typically been at a level of one-fifth or less of annual imports. When compared with the figures taken as representing the respective countries' liquidities, these data yield ratios which indicate liquidities corresponding to several years' requirements.

Although this improved ratio is distinctly superior to the reserves-to-imports ratio, it has some of the latter's defects as well as some of its own. For example, although the net balance in the external accounts is a smaller magnitude, it is a residual and is highly variable. For Germany during the years 1953 through 1962, the net external balance varied from an arithmetic figure as low as $163 million to one of $1,684 million; for Italy, the range was from $8 million to $804 million. As a result, the liquidity ratios for these two countries (which are not extreme examples among the Ten) showed a variation of considerable range. For Germany the values varied from less than 3 to 49, although in seven out of the ten years the liquidity volume lay in the range of 4 to 7 times the overall external balance.

This variability in the ratio liquidity-to-net external balance, which results from the wide shifts in the size of the external balance itself, has a further related effect which is as initially disconcerting as it is mathematically inevitable. When the net external balances are very small the ratio under consideration assumes very high values, and when the balance of payments approaches equilibrium the liquidity ratio approaches infinity. At first glance, this may appear absurd or at

9

least unmanageable for operating with problems, but on reflection it is seen to vindicate, in one sublime mathematical truism, the validity of the liquidity-to-net balance ratio as the fundamental measure of "adequacy." That is, where the balance of payments is fully in equilibrium, there is no drawing down of a country's liquidity and the volume of that liquidity is unlimited (i.e., infinite) with reference to functional requirements. (When it comes to working with statistical calculations of this liquidity ratio in practice, it would appear advisable, in generalizing or averaging, to ignore the extreme values and work ordinarily with figures reflecting modal values.)

In working with the ratio liquidity-to-net external balance, another difficulty arises from the fact that a country's net external payments may show either a positive or a negative balance. How should positive and negative values in the external balance be regarded conceptually in their relation to a country's liquidity; and how should these plus and minus balances be treated statistically in computing the ratios used in approaching the "adequacy" question? In arguing the advantages of a ratio which compares liquidity to the net external balance, the presentation has consciously employed the case of a country with a negative balance in its payments. It is in such cases that the monetary authorities' liquidity resources will be called upon. Indeed, the definition adopted at the outset of this paper is explicitly couched in terms which are at least apparently functional when it defines liquidity as resources ". . . available . . . for the purpose of financing temporary deficits . . ." It might be argued that liquidity serves no purpose except for financing a deficit or protecting a weak currency, and this view rigidly followed might lead to the conclusion that the ratio liquidity-to-net external balance is of little interest except in those cases in which the denominator is negative. This line of thought, by the way, would establish a parallel between the ratio of liquidity to net balance and the ratio of liquidity to imports: although the value of imports is not shown as a negative figure in a time series on annual imports, of course, it always has a minus value in the algebra of the balance of payments.

The questions posed in the preceding paragraph about how to regard plus and minus values in the net external balance are answered by the present author by concluding that both types of imbalance should be considered and that they should be treated relatively alike. Either a deficit or a surplus on this year's balance of external payments will affect the volume of liquidity and, hence, its adequacy relative to some existing or assumed level of requirements. We can perhaps speak with more certainty about *changes* in the adequacy of a country's liquid resources than about whether a certain volume is "adequate." Even if we were to start with the assumption that today a given country's liquidity is "less than adequate," an increase (through next year's payments surplus) in resources could render its liquidity "less inadequate" than before. A country which generates a balance-of-payments deficit of a given size is not unlikely to produce a surplus of the same general order of magnitude. Because of various factors of structure and policy, there is likely to be some rough comparability in amplitude, in absolute terms, of plus and minus swings for a given country. If there were only a few countries in the world and one of them were having a payments deficit, one or more of the remainder would be having a surplus and total payments in that little world would equal receipts. If it is meaningful to compare the first country's liquidity with its net external negative imbalance, it is probably also valid to compare the second country's liquidity with its net positive imbalance. Finally and half facetiously, if the relationship of liquidity to net payments imbalance can only be conceived and computed when the latter is negative, there would be no measurement available for many Group of Ten countries for most of the past decade. In the liquidity ratios computed for Group of Ten countries, the ratio is calculated regardless of sign, but those in which the balance was negative are asterisked.

Only one further point will be commented on briefly in this general review of the ratio liquidity-to-net external balance—namely, the question *which* balance? Conceivably, a country's external liquidity could be compared with one or another of the various partial or sub-balances in the balance of payments: the trade balance, current-account balance, "basic balance," balance excluding governmental capital transactions, etc. It seems clear, however, that if it is meaningful to construe an imbalance in a country's international payments as measuring, in some acceptable sense, a "requirement" against which to compare its available monetary resources, then it is surely the net overall balance which must be chosen as most relevant to any consideration of the adequacy of the country's liquidity.

IV. THE STATISTICAL RECORD

In the preceding section, we commenced examining the subject of the adequacy of liquidity by looking qualitatively at the notion of computing a ratio of liquidity, and attention was centered on some of the general attributes of the pertinent variables: the owned or available monetary resources which constitute liquidity, and the latter's relation to imports, to the net external balance, etc. There are more comments to be made on this subject of the general validity of the standard "liquidity ratio" as a measure of the adequacy of such monetary resources and on the possible future behavior of that relationship. Before returning to pursue these subjects, however, it would be useful first to examine the statistical record to see what the experience of the Group of Ten countries has been and what are the orders of magnitude involved in the liquidity question.

The material presented herein consists of one table and one chart for each of the Group of Ten member countries (plus Switzerland). These country tables and charts, appearing in the Annex, give annual data for the ten-year period 1953-1962 on the following: Total liquidity available to the monetary authority; a breakdown of this total "official" liquidity into its main components of owned reserves and credit availability; the volume of imports; the net external balance on international payments; the two computed ratios of liquidity adequacy discussed above.

There appear to be good *a priori* reasons for concentrating attention on the Group of Ten (always, for present purposes, the Ten plus Switzerland). As stated at the beginning, these reasons include the general similarity in behavior of these economically advanced countries, the fact that through their mutual undertakings they have constituted themselves a somewhat distinct Group, and the fact that taken together they account for more than seven-tenths of liquidity held by all countries.[7] Whether these countries are in fact highly homogeneous will perhaps become somewhat clearer through the data to be examined.

The statistics used herein are all taken from standard series compiled by international institutions. Since the series and their sources are identified and explained to the extent necessary in the Annex, no explanations need be given in the text, with the one major exception of the series on liquidity. For each country, the volume of total liquidity most closely approximating our accepted definition is taken to be

[7] For reasons which are more than esthetic, this circumlocution of "liquidity held by all countries" is somewhat less objectionable than a foreshortened term like "world liquidity," though any complete aggregation of liquidity, however termed, has only limited meaning.

measured by the sum of its official gross holdings of gold and (convertible) foreign currencies plus its "total-tranche position" in the International Monetary Fund. (In addition, for the last two dates of the period covered, the total liquidity is shown both exclusive and inclusive of amounts available to the monetary authority under existing bilateral swap agreements.) There can be no quarrel about the inclusion of gold and foreign-currency holdings (i.e., the standard measure of "official reserves" or "owned liquidity"), and the only question which arises is the propriety of any measure taken of the credit component or non-owned liquidity. The I.M.F. itself, by yielding in 1963 to the idea of publishing a series on liquidity, stopped one step short of the measure advocated above. In the Fund tables, a series made up of the sum of official reserves and the Fund gold-tranche position is given in a table labeled "Total Reserves." There is some presumption that the Fund regards "total reserves" so defined as being synonymous with "total liquidity," although in the same section on "international liquidity" in *International Financial Statistics* it publishes the figures on each country's total-tranche position as well as those on its gold-tranche position.[8] Having regard for the policies and practices of the I.M.F., the author tends to consider that for any Group of Ten member the total tranche (i.e., its gold-tranche position plus that additional amount which it might draw from the Fund "if its justification were sufficient, without waiver of the limitation of 200 per cent of quota on Fund holdings") should be regarded as a credit resource readily available to the monetary authority in the sense of our liquidity definition. The inclusion of the full amount of the total tranche rather than the gold portion thereof makes only a small difference in the *general level* of the liquidity measure and in most instances the movements of the curve are not affected.

What light can the statistical record shed on the absolute and relative amounts of external liquidity held by financially significant countries?

1. The period 1953-1962 was one of substantial and sustained growth in the liquidity, in absolute terms, available to the eleven countries of the Group under study. The nine non-reserve-currency countries expanded their liquidity position from about $13 billion in 1953 to about $31 billion in 1962.

[8] The total-tranche position of an I.M.F. member is defined as follows: "The sum of the Gold Tranche and Credit Tranche Positions, i.e., twice the member's quota minus the Fund's holdings of the member's currency." *International Financial Statistics* (December 1963), p. 7.

2. Although all nine countries registered significant gains, there were marked differences in the percentage increases among countries, explained in part by the different levels of reserve depletion occasioned by World War II from which they started. France and Germany increased their liquidity levels about 3½ times between 1953 and 1962, whereas Sweden's increase barely amounted to 1½ times.

3. For the eleven countries as a whole, the period was, as is well known, a time of redistribution as well as of increase. In the United Kingdom, gross official liquidity rose from $3.9 billion to $5.3 billion, and in the United States it declined from $26.2 billion to $21.4 billion.[9]

4. The composition of the liquidity available to the monetary authorities in the nine non-reserve-currency countries underwent a change. The credit component of total liquidity resources about doubled in many cases, and for some of the larger Continental countries the increase was greater. Nevertheless, some of the same non-reserve-currency countries were also experiencing an even larger rise in gold and foreign-exchange holdings. For the nine countries taken together, the credit component remained almost the same proportion (just under one-fifth) of total liquidity as in 1953. For both the reserve-currency nations, the credit component became a larger proportion of total liquidity.

5. Not only was the period one of generally rising liquidity levels for the non-reserve-currency countries but it was, to a lesser extent, also one without wide fluctuations. Exceptions were the rather sharp 1957 dip in Japanese liquidity, and the successive French financial difficulties in 1956-1957. Minor declines were temporarily experienced by Canada and the Netherlands.[10]

6. In those rather few cases in which a Group of Ten country has been under heavy balance-of-payments pressure, it has been common

[9] In this section, attention will be concentrated mainly on the data for the non-reserve currency countries.

[10] The development of liquidity during this or any other period would describe a more uneven curve, of course, if the monthly rather than year-end figures were used. In some respects it would be preferable to show monthly figures, either the actual data or a moving average. However, there are strong reasons for not doing so. We are not primarily concerned with a precise statistical analysis of any given country situation but with using the data to provide a numerical frame of comparison. Moreover, since one of the questions to be examined is the adequacy of liquidity relative to various commonly assumed requirements such as imports or the net external-payments balance—balance-of-payments phenomena which do not conform to periodicities as short as a month—it seems better on the whole not to employ monthly series, statistical smoothing, or seasonal adjustments.

for its monetary authority, in cooperation with the I.M.F., to allow a large, and often greater than *pari passu*, portion of the deficit to fall temporarily upon the credit component of its liquidity. This occurred in the United Kingdom in 1956-1957 and to a greater extent in 1961.

7. Total imports into the Group were rising throughout the period. Imports by the nine non-reserve-currency countries more than doubled from about $32 billion in 1953 to $65.5 billion in 1962. The rate of increase was somewhat lower in the United States and it was considerably lower in Canada and the United Kingdom.

In order to examine the adequacy of liquidity available to the countries of the Group of Ten, it is necessary to look at the ratios or relationships for countries individually; aggregations of imports or monetary liquidity have limitations enough, but these would be compounded if ratios were computed from the aggregates. The requirement of any country for liquidity is determined with reference to its own balance-of-payments constellation, rather than with reference to some aggregate or average.

8. The countries under examination appear to have some individual characteristics with respect to the ratio between liquidity and imports. In Switzerland, for example, external liquidity has fluctuated around a high level 1.0 to 1.2 times Swiss annual imports. In the Netherlands, the ratio of liquidity to imports has varied in the range 0.40 to 0.50, whereas in Germany and Italy the level is typically higher.

9. Despite individual differences among countries in the typical ratio of liquidity to imports and despite variations from time to time for any one country, the Group of Ten countries displayed in the period 1953-1962 a level of liquidity generally well above the 35 per cent of imports which Professor Triffin found to be the average *reserve* level reached in 1957 by *all* countries outside the United States and United Kingdom.[11]

10. With regard to secular trend, there is no high uniformity in the movement experienced during this period by the different countries in their ratios of external liquidity to imports. About half of them (Canada, Belgium, Germany, Japan, and perhaps the Netherlands) ended the period with roughly the same liquidity-to-imports relationship as

[11] *Gold and the Dollar Crisis, op.cit.*, pp. 40-46. Triffin, although recognizing differences between individual countries and between the major trading countries and the less-developed world, nevertheless regarded 35 per cent of imports in *owned reserves* as "on the low side of any reasonable estimate of world *liquidity requirements*" by countries outside the United Kingdom and United States (*ibid.*, p. 46; italics not in original).

at the beginning. In Italy and France the ratio tended to rise during the period, whereas in Switzerland and Sweden there was some decline. The movement which Triffin, working only with figures on owned reserves, thought he detected as a general decline "at a rather alarming pace"[12] from the end of 1954 to the end of 1957 affected temporarily some of the Group of Ten but was thereafter reversed.

11. For this group of countries, it is also not possible to discern any identifiable trend as compared with earlier (pre-1950) times. The data for earlier years presented by the I.M.F. study and elsewhere relate to owned reserves only, and the years chosen for comparison are so widely separated and subject to so many special factors that no conclusions on trend would be safe.[13]

We turn now, in these summary observations on the figures for the Group of Ten, to the other relative measure of liquidity adequacy which, as discussed earlier in Section III, was seen to be of at least equal interest, namely, the ratio of liquidity to the net external-payments balance.

12. Owing to the inherent general characteristics of the ratio of liquidity to net external balance which were discussed on pp. 9-10 in Chapter III above (characteristics resulting largely from the fact that the net external balance of a country is a residual which can vary from zero up to a substantial figure), there are wide variations in this series of ratios. The highly volatile values of this ratio, which are produced at the upper end of the range when the payments balance is approximately in equilibrium, must be ignored and attention concentrated on the modal values.

13. For the non-reserve-currency countries, there were only two instances in which any country's year-end liquidity was so low that it no more than equalled the volume of its net external-balance-of-payments deficit for the year. There were only six other instances in which a country's liquidity was less than three times its net external balance. In a substantial proportion of the 85 cases, the country had external liquidity in the range of four to ten times the size of its overall net payments balance for the year involved.

14. What trend, if any, characterized this ratio over the ten-year period? We have noted above that the liquidity held by countries in this Group was rising during the period, more for some countries than

[12] *Ibid.*, p. 40.
[13] I.M.F., *International Reserves and Liquidity*. For a good exposition of the difficulties in comparing with the 1930's and earlier periods, see Triffin, *op.cit.*, pp. 38-40.

for others. Whether the value of the ratio would rise or fall depended, obviously, on whether the rising level of the numerator (liquidity volume) was matched by a corresponding rise in the denominator (net external balance). The outcome for different members of the Group of Ten was not at all uniform. Without discussing each of the nine individually, we should note a few differing cases.

In Germany, the ratio of liquidity to net external balance rose only slowly and slightly over the period as a whole, with a somewhat greater rise in the latter years. This resulted from a rather steadily rising liquidity volume, a large and growing payments surplus in the early and middle years, and a leveling-off and fall in the payments balance in the late years. The ratio for France, on the other hand, started to decline, reached in 1957 the lowest value for any of the countries, and after 1959 rose strongly. France's low ratios for 1956 and 1957 reflected both her drawing-down of reserves and of I.M.F. credits and the appearance of substantial payments deficits. Switzerland, whose liquidity started from a high volume and less than doubled during the ten years, had a ratio to net external balance which fluctuated at a comfortably high level, with perhaps some tendency downward after 1957.

Insofar as one can summarize the individual results, it would appear that in seven of the nine non-reserve-currency countries of the Group of Ten, the ratio of liquidity to the country's net external balance either rose over the course of the period or remained roughly the same.

15. In the countries with reserve currencies, we see that the United Kingdom's external liquidity did not fall below 6 times her net external-payments balance and (extremely high values ignored) usually amounted to 8-12 times the external balance. The trend, insofar as any existed, seemed to be slightly upward toward the end of the period. For the United States, the persistent balance-of-payments deficit during the late 1950's and early 1960's produced a decline during the ten-year period in the ratio of liquidity to net external balance.

V. MEANING OF ADEQUACY: A RECONSIDERATION

Although the relationship described by the ratio of a country's total external liquidity to its net external-payments balance does constitute a more meaningful measurement of the "adequacy," from a functional standpoint, of liquidity than the more habitual one of liquidity (or of reserves) to imports, both measures leave much to be desired as an explanation of developments in the past ten years and possibly also as an explanation of what one may expect to occur in the future. These limitations arise from several reasons.

First, the data presented primarily measure *changes* in liquidity. Figures are available which conform in a fairly acceptable manner to our definition of the volume of "external liquidity," and it is possible to measure variations in the absolute level of liquidity for any member of the Group of Ten. Moreover, if a country's net external-payments balance (or, if that is still preferred by some, the value of its imports) is taken as representing the "requirements" against which liquidity is desired to be available, it is likewise possible to trace the changes in the adequacy of the liquidity available to the monetary authority by means of a series of ratios between the two magnitudes. That series for any country does not indicate of itself, however, whether the level of liquidity at the beginning or end of the period, as measured by the ratio, was adequate in any absolute sense. The recent Brookings study wrestled briefly with the fact of this lack of any "objective definition" of the adequacy of monetary reserves, abandoned the search, and fell back on the subjective judgment of the monetary authorities of the various countries as to whether their respective reserves were adequate or not.[14] (The conclusions to which this approach led with respect to the adequacy of present reserves will be noted subsequently.)

What occurred during the post-war period up through 1963 was that a substantial accumulation of liquidity was registered by most countries of the Group of Ten. Liquid external resources grew rapidly in absolute terms for the nine non-reserve-currency countries, with some accompanying shift in world distribution of these resources as a result of reductions in United States liquidity levels. During the 1950's and early 1960's, rising reserves owned by the monetary authorities were also supplemented by the establishment of fairly large credit facilities readily available to the monetary authorities through the I.M.F. This growth of liquidity of the nine was effected partly by a conscious rebuilding of reserve holdings depleted during or just after World War II, a rebuilding which was financed in part by direct transfers of economic assistance. To a much greater extent, however, it was the result of, or obverse side of, successive deficits in the U.S. balance of payments. That is, growth in official holdings of external liquidity by the Group of Ten countries (other than the United States) occurred

[14] See Walter S. Salant and associates, *The U.S. Balance of Payments in 1968* (Washington: The Brookings Institution, 1963), pp. 234-235.

to a considerable extent not only because of any consciously held "reserve policy" as such, but also because of their general economic policies of recovery and stabilization of which external monetary policy formed a part, as well as because of a combination of international factors such as the pattern of world trade and payments, the course of raw commodity prices, a U.S. balance-of-payments deficit characterized by a high volume of private investment abroad and large outlays for military and economic assistance, and the necessity for the developing countries to spend virtually the whole of their foreign-exchange receipts.

Stating the matter in another fashion, the rising levels of liquidity exhibited by the nine countries largely reflected the fact that during the period their external-payments balances were preponderantly in surplus.[15] (Of the 85 individual balances for the nine countries, 67 were positive balances.) The experiences of individual countries differed somewhat, and for some members of the Group of Ten the recorded surpluses were substantial in amount. Thus, for a few members of the Group the ratio of liquidity to net external balance rose somewhat over the period; and for at least some of the cases in which the liquidity ratio did not rise the explanation was that the external balance itself was relatively large. Moreover, the relative level of liquidity was being either maintained or increased in the respective countries not in comparison with a net external balance which was in deficit but with one which was typically in varying degrees of surplus.

As a part of the examination of changes in the adequacy of external liquidity, it is desirable to look now at a constituent matter: namely, the trends in the net external-payments balance itself. Have there been changes in the size of the net external imbalance of a given member of the Group of Ten? Has the external-payments balance changed in relation to the country's total international transactions? It seems important to inquire what were the experiences of the Group of Ten countries in these respects during the period 1953-1962, for some writers have formulated assumptions or hypotheses about how these relationships (and hence the requirements for liquidity) may develop in the future. Regrettably, the period 1953-1962 is not sufficiently long or "typical"—what period is?—but at this moment we cannot extend it at either end.

[15] Increased amounts of credits readily available through the I.M.F. also contributed to the rising liquidity levels.

First, as to the changes in the net external balance. In several Group of Ten countries, the magnitude of the net balance (disregarding plus or minus signs) appears to have remained approximately the same during the period, with no pronounced trend. This could be said for Belgium, Canada, France, Japan, Sweden, and perhaps Netherlands.[16] For each of those countries there were indeed fluctuations, but the absolute size of the net balance did not appear to have any persistent tendency to rise or fall. In two other countries—Italy and Switzerland —the absolute size of the net balance grew somewhat in the period 1958-1960. In both countries, a reduction had occurred by the end of 1961; but it would nevertheless appear accurate to say that, with respect to the period 1953-1962 as a whole, there was a rise in the absolute size of the net external balance of both countries. (For Italy and Switzerland, the rise in absolute size also constituted a fairly large increase of the surplus in percentage terms.) The remaining non-reserve-currency country, Germany, showed a decrease in the absolute size of its net external balance. As for the reserve-currency countries, the United Kingdom's net balances displayed no noticeable trend during the period. In the United States, the imbalances were higher during the years 1958-1960, although they declined after 1960, and no clear trend appears.[17] To summarize, two or possibly three of the eleven countries under review showed some increase in the absolute size of their net foreign balances within the ten-year period, though some of these fell again; and the majority of countries in the Group showed a stable or declining trend.

To compare a country's net payments balance with its total international transactions is difficult statistically. Even for the generally statistically oriented members of the Group of Ten, no acceptable series are available. The aggregation of "total international transactions" is, even apart from measurement problems, a matter not at all free from conceptual ambiguities when one leaves the merchandise-trade account and enters the current-invisibles or the capital sections of the balance of payments. Nevertheless, with these reservations, one or two very rough approximations can be attempted of the *rate of increase* in total international transactions.

[16] Note that we are not saying anything at this point to compare countries within this sub-group with one another as to either the magnitude or algebraic sign of their respective balances.

[17] This seems to hold true both for the O.E.C.D. series and the more familiar Department of Commerce series. See Salant and associates, *op.cit.*, Appendix Table 1, pp. 278-281.

The first of these could be found by assuming that the "growth of international transactions in goods and services" for the world as a whole, as estimated in one unpublished study for a period in the 1950's, also measures the growth of international transactions for the Group of Ten. Salant and associates cite one finding[18] that total goods-and-services transactions grew during the period 1950-1952 to 1956-1958 at an average annual rate of 6.2 per cent. If that rate of 6.2 per cent per year is assumed to hold over the nine-year period from 1953 to 1962, the world total of international transactions in goods and services would have grown by 72 per cent. It might then be assumed that each of the Group of Ten countries might likewise have experienced a 72-per-cent growth in such international transactions.

There is reason to believe, however, that international transactions of countries in the Group of Ten may have grown more rapidly than those of the entire world. When the rates of increase in either exports or imports for these advanced countries are compared with the rates for the world, they are seen to be generally higher than the latter. A second estimate of the growth in total transactions can be hazarded by assuming that, for each country of the Group, its total international transactions expanded at the same rate as its total merchandise trade.[19] Under the assumption, temporarily adopted, that growth in total merchandise trade during the period 1953-1962 was accompanied by a roughly equivalent growth in total international transactions, the data do support the supposition that these total transactions of Group of Ten countries grew more rapidly than those estimated for the world as a whole. Except for three countries (Canada, United Kingdom, and United States), the total merchandise trade of each member of the Group of Ten increased by figures ranging from 90 to about 200 per cent, well over the 72 per cent increase estimated for the entire world.

Whatever the defects in these two very rough estimates of the increase in international transactions, it seems highly probable that the true increase in this value must have been substantial. During that period, rising economic activity and the liberalization of governmental policies affected both trade and invisible transactions on current account; and if private capital transactions were more slowly liberalized

[18] From an "unpublished and preliminary manuscript by Herbert B. Woolley," Salant and associates, *op.cit.*, p. 239.

[19] Since no refined estimates seemed possible for the limited use that could be made of them, the following simple method was employed. Exports f.o.b. and imports c.i.f. for 1953 were added together for each country and the total compared with the corresponding total for 1962.

they were also supplemented by large governmental transfers. If we take the lower of the two estimates, we can assume that each of the Group of Ten increased its total international transactions by about 72 per cent from 1953 to 1962. If it is recalled that, for most of the Group, the absolute size of the net external balance had a stable or declining trend during the period, it seems possible to conclude, even from these imprecise data, that the net external-payments balance typically represented a *declining* percentage of total international transactions for those advanced countries which were the preponderant holders of external monetary liquidity.

Having observed some of the facts about changes in the levels of liquidity experienced by leading countries and about changes in such liquidity levels relative to net external-payments balances, it would be well now, before closing this review of present adequacy, to return very briefly to the idea of "subjective" standards of adequacy, espoused by the Salant study. As noted earlier, Salant and associates adopted as one of their fundamental assumptions that "present reserves are no more than adequate" and based this assumption not on any objective measure—which they regarded as nonexistent—but on the subjective view held by the various monetary authorities that their reserves were inadequate. "We need not pass judgment on whether the subjective reactions of monetary authorities are justified. It is sufficient to take their reactions as data . . ." This decision related to reserves, rather than all forms of liquidity as defined in the present paper, and it was a summarization of the world situation, rather than exclusively that of Group of Ten countries. Nevertheless, the Brookings authors did proceed to apply their conclusion explicitly to the latter countries, saying that "although some European countries apparently feel comfortable . . . there is no evidence that they regard their reserves as more than adequate or that they would not be constrained by their reserve positions if faced with deficits."[20]

Citation of the foregoing opinion should be taken neither as indicating an agreement with the monetary authorities' judgment about the barely adequate condition of their reserve position nor as a concurrence in the decision of the Brookings authors that the subjective judgment of the monetary authorities must be accepted. The purpose of the citation was rather the following. The topic under examination in this sub-section is the adequacy of liquidity in the present and recent past. The quantitative measurements found thus far pertain largely

[20] *Op.cit.*, pp. 234-235.

to *changes* in the liquidity relationship, in the absence of any accepted standard as to what the absolute level of the coefficient of liquidity should be, in general or in a specific instance, in order to qualify as "adequate." If the numerical or objective measurements provide an incomplete standard, the subjective judgment—which pronounces the undifferentiated conclusion of "inadequate" upon the reserve positions of both the underdeveloped countries and the advanced countries and which, with regard to the latter, can apply the term with little distinction between 1961-1963 and earlier periods—does not offer even the possibility of measuring changes. We mention it in passing here, both because it provides another view of liquidity adequacy contrasting with, or additional to, the more quantitative appraisal given above; and because this anxious subjective judgment—the insecure feeling that no level of liquidity achieved is adequate—forms part of the psychological foundation from which the whole professional inquiry into the "liquidity problem" has proceeded.

Prospective changes in the adequacy of liquidity: the current opinion.

To those who have been concerned with the "liquidity problem," the major preoccupation has been with regard to its future adequacy: that is, with regard to the possibilities that the liquidity position of the major countries is and will continue to become progressively more inadequate. Since that thesis has been clearly expressed and well publicized, it will be sufficient to summarize the main outlines of the argumentation, basing our summary upon the Triffin version and that given by Salant and associates.[21]

According to these authors, the main problem arises from the inability of accretions to the supply of reserves owned by the monetary authorities (gold and foreign currencies) to keep pace with what is believed to be the rate of increase in requirements for such (owned) reserves. More exactly:

1. The requirements for reserves are assumed by Triffin (and by the I.M.F.) to be established by the need to maintain a constant percentage relation to world imports. Since world imports are projected to grow at an average annual rate of 3-6 per cent, and since reserves must grow at a pace no slower than that of total imports, the requirements for reserves will rise correspondingly. (Salant and associates appear to accept the fact that a country's net payments imbalances offer a more

[21] See Triffin, *op.cit.*, pp. 47-50, 35-37; and Salant and associates, *op.cit.*, pp. 237-238 and 234.

relevant indication of reserve requirements than do total imports. Nevertheless, these authors likewise conclude that the requirements for reserves are rising rapidly, owing to their belief that imbalances will increase at least in the same proportion as international transactions, and probably at a greater rate.)

2. Attention is confined by Triffin and Salant to the reserves owned by the monetary authorities, rather than to the more broadly defined total external liquidity. Except for an occasional passing phrase,[22] the credit component of external liquidity is omitted by these authors from the analysis and the measurement of the existing system.

3. The reserve holdings under the existing gold-exchange standard consist principally of gold and convertible currencies, mainly dollars. The supply of monetary gold is increasing at too slow a rate. The United States balance-of-payments deficit is being reduced, and when equilibrium has been restored there will no longer be a net source of dollars to add annually to world reserves.

4. Since the monetary gold stock is increasing at a rate less rapid than the requirements mentioned in 1. above are presumed to increase, there emerges, according to this view, a progressively critical liquidity problem.

Prospective changes in the adequacy of liquidity: a modified view

The thesis of a progressively deteriorating liquidity position for the advanced nations of the world, summarized in the immediately preceding paragraphs, can now be modified in the light of the analytical considerations presented in this paper. The question of whether a country's external liquidity is "adequate" and the question of what changes may occur in that adequacy are matters involving both the requirements for and the supply of liquidity resources; and the materials examined in this paper suggest the need for recasting the current view in both respects.

Let us start with the role assigned to the U.S. balance of payments. It is accepted[23] that equilibrium will be progressively restored and that, except for occasional fluctuations, the United States will achieve international balance. One effect of that evolution would, of course, be that the rate of net increase in the world's supply of dollar reserves would fall substantially. The theory posits that liquidity requirements are growing rapidly, being determined either directly by the trend

---

22 See, for example, Salant and associates, *op.cit.*, bottom of p. 234.
23 E.g., see Salant and associates, *op.cit.*, pp. 238-240.

of world imports or indirectly by another more complex relationship. A return toward equilibrium by the United States would also have the consequence, however, that the payments surpluses of other countries, including especially the leading countries in the Group of Ten, would be reduced.[24] This fact, which tends to be neglected by current writers on liquidity, acquires immediate significance if it is now recognized that it is these very net payments imbalances that are relevant to determining liquidity requirements (and, hence, liquidity adequacy).

This relationship between a changed or changing level of dollar deficits and the liquidity situation of the other major financial nations deserves careful attention. Let us take as an assumption, for simplicity, the same situation posited in the Salant study, namely that the international payments of the United States will have reached equilibrium (i.e., as an average position) by 1968. Let us further assume that, correspondingly, the payments surpluses of some other members of the Group of Ten are reduced by an amount totaling (among them) a roughly similar figure. The aspect of this situation which has been customarily noted is that the *net* flow of dollars arising from current U.S. balance-of-payments deficits would have ceased for the group as a whole (though not necessarily for individual countries). That is correct. It is equally correct, however, that the payments imbalances, which constitute the functional purpose that external liquidity resources are designed to serve, would likewise have been reduced. During the period of falling dollar deficits and falling (average) surpluses of other countries, the typical Group of Ten country would discover that the ratio of its liquidity to its net external-payments balance was rising. Whatever uncertainty there may always be about what absolute coefficient of liquidity is safe or appropriate or adequate, the volume of liquidity of the country in question would become greater (i.e., more adequate) in relation to the diminishing or diminished magnitude of its payments imbalance.

In the preceding paragraph, the account given of a rather steadily declining net external surplus was, of course, generalized and oversimplified. Can anything more precise be said about the probable prospective evolution of the liquidity situation of the major countries? Remembering always that liquidity "adequacy" is only meaningful with respect to the supply-requirement relation of each particular country or monetary area taken individually, can we foresee anything

[24] The phrasing of this sentence does not necessarily imply, of course, that any one country's balance of payments is *the* independent variable.

at all about how the liquidity resources and requirements of a typical Group of Ten country may evolve?

First, the prospective trend of liquidity requirements. Salant and associates took as an assumption "that future imbalances in world payments, which give rise to the need for reserves to settle net balances, will rise at least in proportion to the future growth of international transactions."[25] (Their view leads to a conclusion generally similar to the conclusion of those who believe that total imports provide an acceptable yardstick for measuring liquidity adequacy.) Now there exist no usable data on the value of total international transactions. Therefore, we are in ignorance as to what the percentage relationship has been, at any given date, in any one of the advanced countries under consideration, between the volume of its external liquidity and the volume of its total international transactions. What we have been able to do in this paper, however, is to tabulate the net external imbalances of each country by years, and to make rough estimates as to the *rate of growth* in its total foreign transactions in those years.

What we found does not necessarily disprove the Salant hypothesis about the future evolution, but our material at least shows that the factual history in the period 1953-1962 differs in important respects from that hypothesis. The countries of the Group of Ten experienced substantial net payments imbalances in many cases during that period, as well as in the earlier post-war years, but for most of the countries these imbalances showed no pronounced upward trend even in their arithmetic size, let alone in their relationship to the country's liquidity resources. And with regard to their relation to total international transactions, the net payments imbalances seemed clearly to represent a diminishing percentage of the respective country's total transactions, rather than the contrary.[26]

Even in the absence of any supporting evidence from the statistical experience of the recent past, the hypothesis of strongly rising future requirements for liquidity might still, of course, be capable of proof by theoretical means. The theoretical case appears to divide into two main portions: that net imbalances are closely related to total transactions volume; and, that imbalances will become larger, relatively speaking. These propositions will be examined briefly.

[25] *Op.cit.*, pp. 235-236. Indeed, they regarded it as a "probability" that future imbalances would become larger relative to total international transactions than in the past.
[26] See pp. 20-21 above.

The better-known writings on liquidity unfortunately make little attempt to prove their assumption that the conditions for maintaining the adequacy of liquidity are defined by a relatively constant percentage relationship between total imports or total international transactions, on the one hand, and total monetary reserves, on the other. Triffin candidly admits that his "main reason" for using total annual imports as a measure of reserve adequacy was the convenient existence of the ready-made calculations. His secondary reason was "that this ratio is the one that has been most popularized in all postwar discussions of the subject," and he asserted that monetary authorities "are apt to think today of reserve adequacy in these terms, and to act accordingly."[27] Similarly, the I.M.F., which had made the calculations Triffin employed, had computed the growth of monetary reserves which would be required over a given span of years to prevent a decline of world reserves in relation to world imports without demonstrating why such an equal percentage growth seemed reasonable to assume.[28] The Brookings authors do indeed recognize that requirements for external liquidity are primarily determined by net payments imbalances. They make no attempt, however, to demonstrate their assumption that these payments imbalances would rise "in proportion to the future growth of international transactions."[29]

Although they take it as a safe minimum assumption that net imbalances in external payments will rise by at least the same percentage rate as total international transactions, the Brookings authors conclude that in the future annual imbalances will be larger, relative to international transactions, than in the past. This they endeavor to verify by examining a number of facts and considerations. Unfortunately, the attempt is not very successful. Many of the factors cited—like greater freedom from trade restrictions, narrowing of the gaps between Europe and America in technology and per capita income, freer flow of long-term capital—may well contribute to an increase in the volume of international transactions, but do not necessarily increase the disequilibria in payments balances. Their other considerations are more relevant

[27] Op.cit., p. 36. Note that Triffin's "own preference" would have been, he said, for using the ratio of reserves to total balance-of-payments receipts on current account—a relationship which does not differ much conceptually from that involved in the ratio to imports and which he also apparently assumed to require pari passu percentage increases.

[28] International Reserves and Liquidity, pp. 69-75.

[29] Op.cit., p. 236. This is distinct from the attempt which they do make, noted below, to show that imbalances might grow at an even higher rate than total transactions.

but also inconclusive. They believe that imbalances caused by differences in cyclical fluctuations between countries or by differences in the respective policy responses to them are likely to diminish, because of the growing policy coordination. Likewise, they surmise that disparate movements in prices will be limited by the "widening of the spectrum of traded goods." Nevertheless, they believe that imbalances due to structural changes are likely to increase in importance, and they tend somewhat uncertainly to conclude that, all factors considered, net payments imbalances probably will rise relative to total international transactions.

Having regard to the inconclusiveness of the Salant-Triffin theory of rapidly mounting future net payments imbalances (= liquidity requirements), it seems desirable to regard their case as not yet fully demonstrated, and to see whether there are additional considerations bearing on the question of future liquidity requirements.[30] This same feeling about the not wholly convincing character of the theoretical foundation of the prognosis is reinforced by the failure of the hypothesis to conform to the statistical record experienced by Group of Ten countries in the 1950's and early 1960's. As noted in this paper, the experience of the typical Group of Ten country was that its net payments imbalances, though often of a fairly large magnitude, seemed rather clearly to be declining relative to its total international transactions, rather than increasing.

In attempting a reformulation, we should note that it does appear logical to presume *some* degree of positive correlation, *ex ante*, between the total money value of a country's international transactions and the amplitude of the imbalances which it experiences in external payments. The external-payments balance, constituting a settlement of the net surplus or deficit arising from transactions with other countries, could perhaps be expected to show some growth in average absolute size if the total value of such transactions with the rest of the world grows. (This implies the legitimacy of presuming the existence of some kind of curve, although of course with all the customary assumptions of *ceteris paribus*, instantaneousness, etc.) The question is, how closely the growth in the size of net imbalances will correspond

[30] "But an increase in international commerce does not necessarily require any increase in international liquidity in the short run, and tends to require such an increase only at less than proportionate rates in the long run." J. Herbert Furth, "International Liquidity—Problems and Solutions," *Pennsylvania Business Survey* (November 1963).

to that in total transactions, and this question has not been satisfactorily answered.

There seems to be no necessary reason to expect these two growth rates to correspond in percentage amounts. As noted above, Salant and associates sifted the many conflicting forces likely to be at work over coming years, and their decision rested on confusing sets of contrary economic forces and even upon somewhat contradictory observations.[31] The Brookings study recognizes that economic cooperation and monetary consultation, which have waxed materially among the advanced nations, are likely to produce a diminution in international imbalances from domestic cyclical causes.

One should remember above all that a country's net external balance is under constant observation by its own monetary authority, not only because of the effect of an imbalance upon the country's external position, but also because of its inflationary or deflationary effect upon the domestic economy. The overall net external-payments balance, being a composite algebraic residual, has an element of chance in its exact figure. But it has a highly derived character and is far from being an independent variable. Under conditions of a full-employment policy (complete with wage and price guidelines!) at home and a policy of close international monetary cooperation abroad, the net external balance of an advanced country under the gold-exchange standard is a *managed* phenomenon.[32] Under these conditions, monetary management is likely to have much more impact upon the net foreign balance than upon the total of foreign transactions, for two reasons. First, because the net external surplus or deficit is precisely the object which is central to the monetary authority's foreign policy; and second, because almost any given set of policies which the authority may adopt is very unlikely to affect its foreign receipts and foreign payments in the same direction and degree. We should not fail to note a point in favor of the Salant associates' thesis—which they failed to mention— that as an economy grows in size the arithmetic magnitude of the net payments imbalance it could sustain with the same percentage impact on the domestic economy would, in principle, also grow. Since, however, the authorities have not been happy with the effects of past im-

[31] Imbalances due to cost discrepancies will "remain slow and difficult," but disparities between different national cost levels "which allow imbalances to develop in the first place will be held down." *Op.cit.*, p. 238.

[32] In this connection, recall how much "stretch" there is in the calculation of the "dollar gap" of an aid-receiving country, which depends to an important degree on the amount of gap which donors will finance.

balances, they may not be content merely with maintaining the same relative shock as formerly.

What would be the effect of all this conflicting evidence or speculation about the size of future net imbalances upon the amount of external liquidity required? If net imbalances to be settled internationally could be expected to rise—whether *pari passu* with a country's international transactions or at a lesser rate—there would be at least a first presumption that the means of international settlement would also need to rise. But here one must immediately enter several reservations.

1. The first of these reservations is that, as indicated above, it still seems very much in doubt what the future relative size of an advanced country's payments imbalance may be. The statistical evidence to date does not support the Triffin-Salant hypothesis of a 4-6 per cent annual growth in a country's net payments imbalances. And a theoretical scrutiny of the net effect of the various factual, institutional, and policy influences which may be at work in the future yields inconclusive results.

2. Second, it must be recognized that even if there were a rise in net payments imbalances, any degree of correlation existing between such imbalances and liquidity requirements would also (as noted above with respect to the relationship between total transactions and net imbalances) only be applicable, strictly speaking, on the customary theoretical assumptions of *ceteris paribus*, etc., implicit in the standard instantaneous demand curve. The problem under examination, unfortunately, is of a different (non-static) nature, involving as it does an estimate of what may happen over a period of future years.

3. The third reservation stems from the nature of external liquidity as a means of international settlement. Since some of the data relevant to the study of international payments relationships are lacking (e.g., data on the total foreign transactions of the several countries), it is instructive to consider whether there are some analogues in domestic economics. Although there are no situations in the internal economy which offer anywhere near complete parallels, there are several which embody elements sufficiently analogous to be worth noting. Two of these only will be mentioned here: the domestic money supply and the total (internal) government debt.

The professional reader will think instantly of the differences as well as similarities between the external liquidity resources held or usable by the monetary authority and the internal money supply. The point to bear in mind is that, although there exists some degree of relationship between the quantity of money at a given time and some of the major domestic macroeconomic variables, such as total domestic transactions, GNP, etc., history of recent decades has shown substantial variations, between countries and over time, in the comparative behavior of the quantity of the money supply and such magnitudes as gross national product. One reason for this variation which comes at once to mind is that of fluctuations in velocity. Another factor, about which we do not know enough, is the influence of institutional and administrative innovations which eliminate, create, or obviate transactions themselves (e.g., the spread of various practices for automatic payroll deductions and withholdings, credit-card systems, etc.). Whatever the influence of changing velocity of circulation and other factors, in many of the advanced economies the growth in the quantity of money has differed materially from that of such aggregates as GNP. Would it then be safe to exclude the possibility that similar changes, secular or occasional, might also operate in the international sphere, so as to influence the relation on the requirements side of the liquidity equation which, in a complex but not necessarily constant fashion, links the total value of a country's international transactions, the average net imbalance in those transactions, and the quantity of external liquidity?[33]

In this recasting of the analysis of liquidity adequacy, we have so far dealt only with the *requirements* side of the requirements-supply relationship, and it is necessary now to make some observations on the *supply* side. Although it has been mainly in the analysis of require-

[33] The internal debt of the central government likewise has a few aspects which have enough similarity to some attributes of the phenomenon of external liquidity to make a brief analogy suggestive. Changes in the central-government debt reflect a kind of balance of payments between the public and private sectors. The government debt level fluctuates in amount, rising when net governmental outlay exceeds governmental receipts and falling when budget surpluses permit debt to be redeemed. Whether there will be any trend in the public debt depends on many social and economic factors, including the tendency of the private economy to establish macroequilibrium at the point of full employment or at some other level. In the United States, the total volume of debt outstanding has been rising slowly, though the amount relative to GNP has fallen markedly since the 1940's.

Some of the debt is in the form of Treasury bills of short maturity and is constantly bought and sold. Other portions are long-term securities held by financial institutions or individuals. The government also has "standby facilities" of credit at the central bank. There is no question of the government's being asked to redeem or "convert" the entire volume of outstanding debt owed abroad (to the private economy), but any portion of it, represented by individual bills or bonds, is highly liquid to the holder.

ments for liquidity that the prevalent assumptions and conclusions have been most in need of reexamination, the nature and sources of supply of external liquidity also have not been fully understood. These comments can be rather brief, however.

Attention has already been called to the fact that the problem of the adequacy of liquidity has usually been analyzed by comparing the aggregates "world reserves" with "world imports," or some variant on this approach.[34] This approach in itself embodies a grave drawback of aggregation—even if it were granted that the ratio reserves-to-imports were the most relevant one for an individual country—since the concept of external liquidity is compromised and any problems of adequacy are obscured by such global aggregates. We have also observed that the analysis ordinarily has been conducted in terms of official holdings of monetary reserves. Thus, even in those passages in which either the theoretical analysis or the statistical citations have departed from the global basis to that of the individual country, the amount of the country's external liquidity has been regarded in terms of owned reserves only. This has meant that several sources of means of international payment conceivably available to the monetary authority have been left out of account. Among the sources of liquidity supply which can, with greater or less soundness, be considered as available to the monetary authority are the credit facilities available with a minimum of delay or formalities at the I.M.F.; bilateral credits open to one central bank from another; the foreign currency holdings of the private sector, particularly the commercial banks; the credit facilities potentially available abroad to the commercial banks, etc.

In the present paper, the arguments were examined for and against counting these various potential sources within the definition of external liquidity as resources "readily available to its monetary authorities for the purpose of financing temporary deficits in its balance of payments and defending the stability of its rate of exchange." It was found that in some countries and at some times any or all of the above foreign assets or availabilities could become accessible to the monetary authority. For purposes of a general theoretical study of the highly advanced countries, and in the interest of conservative interpretation, the content generally given in this paper to the external liquidity of a country has been the monetary authority's gold, its convertible foreign currencies, and its total-tranche position in the I.M.F. The figures given for each Group of Ten country in the annexed tables for "total

[34] E.g., Triffin, *op.cit.*, pp. 70-73 and 47-58.

official external liquidity" represent the total of the above three components.

Total liquidity thus defined probably constitutes a minimum interpretation for the countries under examination. Employment of this minimum measurement can be defended, as indicated in earlier sections above, both on conceptual grounds because it raises no question of exceeding a rigorous interpretation of credit *readily* available and on grounds of statistical comparability and obtainability because the required figures exist for constructing series for the period 1953-1963. Adoption of even this minimum interpretation of total external liquidity has the effect of raising the whole level of each country's series in contrast to series which omit the I.M.F. credit component entirely (or which, like the Fund's own recently introduced series, include only the country's "gold tranche"). By raising the absolute level of the liquidity figures by the (gradually augmented) credit component, their level compared with the respective series on net external imbalances is likewise somewhat raised, of course.

Above these "minimum" totals for external liquidity there are additional sums which might well qualify as part of the external-liquidity supply for some countries and in some years. A case in point is the credit extended by the European Payments Union in the 1950's. Looked at *ex post*, it is plain that monetary resources did become available to various members of the E.P.U. for financing temporary payments deficits. Depending upon what tranche of its credit quota an E.P.U. debtor was in and upon other circumstances, such financing was generally roughly comparable in automaticity and availability to I.M.F. financing and was sometimes used in conjunction therewith. It might be argued that for European members of the Group of Ten the liquidity series for the years up through 1958 should be adjusted by adding figures on the *unused* credit available to the country through E.P.U. We have been discouraged from doing so not so much by the fact that only a part of the period would be affected and only those series for E.P.U. members as by the practical difficulties in getting consistent series for even that limited period, because of changes in the mechanics of the system. Without elaborating further, it does seem probable that for at least some Group of Ten countries which were also E.P.U. members, the series on liquidity understate available external resources by some (uncomputed) amount of unused E.P.U. facilities.

A second source which is essential to mention is the International

Monetary Fund facilities beyond those embodied in the "total-tranche position" which, as explained earlier, is included for each country in the liquidity data in the Annex. The possibility exists, under given conditions and justifications, for a country to draw an additional amount beyond that reflected in its total-tranche position. In addition, the very Group of Ten countries upon whose liquidity situation this paper is primarily focused have established with the Fund, under the General Arrangements to Borrow adopted in 1962, facilities whereby the Fund can borrow from them and in turn lend to one of their number substantial supplementary amounts. This latter source is of considerable magnitude. However, in this paper no entries were made for either of the two I.M.F. facilities mentioned in this paragraph, both because the conditions attaching to their use might not be fully consistent with a conservative interpretation of resources "readily available" to the monetary authority and because the amount which would be obtainable, assuming the conditions met, is indeterminate in advance.

Another source of liquidity supply which has not generally been included in this paper thus far is that embodied in bilateral credit arrangements. During the past two years, this type of credit facility available to a country's monetary authority has become rather well-known, usually in the form of "swap" arrangements. In the typical case, two central banks agree to establish equivalent mutual credits in favor of each other, with the right of either or both parties to activate the arrangement by a drawing, and with settlement for utilized credits to be effected within a short period.[35] By the end of 1963, the United States had established bilateral arrangements with a number of central banks, mainly those represented in the Group of Ten, aggregating about $2.1 billion, most of which stood available (unutilized). (In the Annex, the table for the United States shows this sum separately and also indicates the effect on the liquidity total for that date of adding the swap figures to other external liquidity.)

It would be legitimate for the years 1962 and 1963 to increase the figures on total liquidity, for the United States and for its respective partners in the swap arrangements, by the amount of such facilities not drawn on those dates. This indicated action has not been done, either in the general tables or in the analytical treatment, in the interest of erring on the side of conservative interpretation under our liquidity

[35] See Charles A. Coombs, "Treasury and Federal Reserve Foreign Exchange Operations," *Federal Reserve Bulletin*, issues of September 1962, and March 1963.

definition. Short-term credit facilities by one central bank for the accommodation of another, though less formalized and less popularly known in the past, have always existed. To include the swap figures in all the tables for 1962 and 1963 might give an exaggerated impression of the increase in liquidity availabilities in the 1960's; and, on the other hand, no estimates seem valid for the amounts of bilateral credits which were potentially available to any Group of Ten country for earlier years. The preferable treatment would appear to apply mental corrections or additions to the future, rather than written ones to the past. In this era of heightened central-bank cooperation, international credits among central banks must be considered increasingly available as a source of liquidity.

The immediately preceding paragraphs reviewed the difference in content between the narrower concept of monetary reserves previously employed in the liquidity literature and the concept of a country's total external liquidity; noted that the content given in this paper to liquidity supply is probably a minimum; and mentioned certain specific sources of monetary resources which, though not easily tallied, might be considered in some cases as forming part of the existing liquidity supply.

Before leaving this subject of supply, it is necessary to observe a significant omission in the customary explanation of the process by which, under the present world monetary system, the existing supply of liquidity is increased. It will suffice to recapitulate[36] this customary exposition by saying that, since liquidity has been treated as comprising only the owned monetary reserves of the given country (or of the "world"), the only streams usually regarded as feeding the supply of liquidity so defined have been (a) accretions to the stock of monetary gold in the Western world by production, Soviet sales, etc., and (b) those increments to the world's holdings of reserve currencies which resulted from an overall net deficit in the balance of payments of the reserve-currency countries during the year in question. This explanation overlooks a source of annual addition to liquidity supply which for many an advanced country is of significant size: the earnings on the monetary authority's foreign assets.

The major financial countries add substantial amounts to their liquidity position annually from earnings on their official holdings of assets abroad, mainly in the form of interest on Treasury bills held in the

[36] See pp. 23-24 above for a fuller summary of the prevailing view of the liquidity-supply process.

reserve centers but also including lesser amounts from other money-market paper, deposit balances, etc. Data published by the German Federal Bank, for instance, show that earnings by that institution from monies employed abroad amounted in 1961 and 1962 to approximately $113 million and $90 million, respectively.[37] When compared to the data in the same annual report on monetary reserves at the close of the two years in question, the interest earnings figures quoted above are the equivalent to 1.75 and 1.42 per cent, respectively, of total reserves.[38] Increments to its liquidity supply from this source by Germany probably are comparatively higher than the average for the Group of Ten, inasmuch as some central banks inexplicably choose to hold a smaller proportion of earning assets.

The important point to observe with respect to this source of increment to a country's liquidity supply is that it does not depend on the continuance of a deficit in the U.S. balance of payments. Nor is it dependent on whether the country holding such interest-earning assets has a surplus in its own balance of payments. Let the matter be stated in this way. Suppose that U.S. external payments will attain equilibrium by 1968 (to take the date adopted by Salant and associates) and continue in approximate average balance. The country whose monetary authority maintains official holdings of Treasury bills and other earning assets in the United States will continue to receive this return regardless of whether its own external payments are in overall balance or not. Looked at from the direction of the United States, achievement of overall equilibrium in the U.S. balance of payments will carry the implication—given the existence of large amounts of dollar income-earning holdings in the hands of foreign monetary authorities—that this item of interest paid to foreign official monetary institutions will be offset by other items in the total balance of payments. The quantitative importance of this accretion to the external liquidity of any given country will depend on various factors, such as the proportion of total liquidity placed in earning assets, the degree of imbalance in its external payments, etc. As one rough or simplified measure of the relative order of magnitude of this factor in relation to other elements, assume that a given country holds no gold whatsoever, that its foreign-currency reserves are entirely invested in American

[37] Deutsche Bundesbank, *Jahresbericht für das Jahr 1962* (Frankfurt), pp. 119 and 131.

[38] Including the gold portion. They would, of course, represent more than 3 per cent of the foreign-currency holdings alone.

and British treasury bills, that the average return on these investments in a given year is, say, 2.5 per cent, and that its balance of payments for that year is in equilibrium. In this simplified case, the country's monetary reserves would increase at an annual rate of 2.5 per cent from this interest factor alone, which compares with the 3 per cent growth rate (I.M.F.) or the 4-6 per cent growth rate (Triffin) in reserves, from *all* sources of supply, which those authors assumed to be required to maintain a constant ratio of reserves to imports.

The foregoing paragraphs on the supply sources of external liquidity are not meant at all to imply an acceptance of the hypothesis in the liquidity literature about the nature and future course of *reserve requirements*—a hypothesis which we found seriously questionable. Rather, these paragraphs are meant to indicate that both the existing supply of liquidity and the means by which it is regularly augmented are greater than previously have been commonly considered.

VI. THE COMPOSITION OF LIQUIDITY

Preceding portions of this paper have discussed the *total amount* of a country's external liquidity, with special reference to the more advanced countries. This is admittedly not the only aspect of the question of whether there is an "adequacy" of liquidity in the world—although it *is* the aspect which has engendered the recent concern about liquidity. Are there other important aspects to the adequacy question? Only two additional ones will be mentioned here, of which the first will not be discussed. This is the position of the less-developed countries with respect to external liquidity. It is a subject for separate discussion —although many of the principles treated here are equally applicable to an understanding of liquidity anywhere—and it must be omitted from the present paper.

The second aspect of the liquidity position of an advanced country, after that of its total value, is the composition of the liquidity resources. The liquidity total comprises the monetary authority's holdings of gold and of convertible-currency assets, plus the additional resources readily available to the monetary authority on credit. Are there considered to be problems, present or forthcoming, with regard to these components and their distribution within a country's total liquidity? In order to isolate the composition from the total magnitude, let us assume that a country's liquidity is adequate in total amount. The discussion then divides into two main cases, depending largely upon the country's balance-of-payments situation.

37

Country in external deficit. If an advanced country is in temporary balance-of-payments deficit of a moderate character, it probably can and will cover its deficit by drawing down its owned reserves of gold and convertible currencies. Either of the two forms will serve the purpose, and the monetary authority may draw proportionately on the two or may elect some other mix, thus changing the relative composition of its reserves in the process. Should the payments deficit be of larger magnitude or longer in duration, the authority may decide to utilize one or more of the credit facilities. If the source chosen is the I.M.F., considerable flexibility of choice is open as to the monetary form in which the credit is drawn, so that no problem of composition is encountered. If some bilateral source is drawn upon, this in any case eases the country's total payments position; and under the conditions of convertibility prevailing among Group of Ten countries, even bilateral drawings under swap agreements can ordinarily be transferred as needed. Although the foregoing treatment is very brief, it does appear accurate in suggesting that an advanced non-reserve-currency country is not likely to have much concern about the composition of its liquidity while running a deficit.[39] It is well to remember that it is only under deficit conditions that a country "uses" it liquidity.

Country in external balance or surplus. When a country's accounts are in balance or in surplus, the composition of its liquidity is sometimes regarded as a problem. Ordinarily the question takes the form of whether the monetary authority is satisfied, at a given moment, with the distribution of its owned reserves: i.e., whether it would prefer a smaller amount or proportion of one or more foreign currencies, and a larger amount of some other currency or of gold. Note that this is not a matter of whether the particular holding will be acceptable in making international payment, since the quality of acceptability is already embraced by the definition of what constitutes external liquidity resources. For the same reason, it also is not a matter of whether the currency held will be available when needed. Finally, as in the case of the country in deficit, the country in surplus or equilibrium is likewise not concerned with the composition of the *credit* component of its liquidity, since the form in which that credit can be

[39] There are occasionally qualifications to this, as when a drawing of one currency from the Fund would inconvenience the country concerned. This problem of composition is more likely to be serious if the deficit is very large and if the country concerned is one of the reserve centers. In that case, however, the problem is more of the size than of the composition of liquidity required.

utilized when needed can be flexibly determined at such future occasion.[40]

Any concern felt by a country over the composition of its owned-reserve holdings, therefore, appears to be a matter related to such questions as the yield, the stability in value, etc., of one or more currencies held.[41] To be sure, a concern over composition occasionally is manifested as an anxiety over the possible devaluation of a reserve currency. The fact that this anxiety is seldom felt outside a few large holders and the fact that the reserve-currency countries have demonstrated the determination and ability to maintain the value of their currencies have shown this fear to be groundless, although it may still repay some academic examination.

The attitude occasionally shown by some central banks toward a potential loss on foreign-currency holdings deserves further study, and the present paper can suggest only a few notes. One causal factor probably is associated with the fact that the modern central bank, however independent it may be of governmental influence in the conduct of a line of monetary policy, is owned by or accountable to the state in some degree for its profits and losses. Central banks and their governments evidently are less worried about making a profit on their foreign assets than about avoiding a loss, for some of them regularly forego interest-earning assets for the safety of holding gold. The attitude sometimes seems to represent less a concern about the size of a potential loss than it does about showing any loss at all for which they might be called to account. Perhaps the central banks should give thought to the feasibility of imitating, in their accounting procedures, the practice of other establishments (including many financial institutions) in setting aside a contingency reserve against this type of potential loss.

In any case, the question of the willingness of the monetary authority of a given advanced country to hold a certain amount of a reserve currency is *not* primarily a part of the problem of external liquidity and its adequacy. We have seen that the problem of adequacy is essentially whether the monetary authority has sufficient monetary resources,

[40] Notwithstanding the accuracy of this as a generalization, there could occasionally be a situation in the I.M.F., after a period of prolonged world-payments disequilibrium, in which there might be a relative scarcity of usable currencies.

[41] For some highly mathematical computations on reserve patterns as well as some very useful remarks about reserve composition, see Peter B. Kenen, *Reserve-Asset Preferences of Central Banks and Stability of the Gold Exchange Standard* (Princeton: Princeton Studies in International Finance No. 10, 1963), pp. 4-9, 64-70.

relative to the size of its net payments imbalances, for settlement abroad; whereas the anxiety of some advanced country with large liquidity resources over the possibility of a onetime fractional loss in value of a part of these resources is a different, and essentially *domestic*, preoccupation. At no time is a reserve-currency country entirely free from the potential peril that a demand of greater or smaller dimensions may be lodged by a foreign monetary authority for conversion of currency reserves into gold. But that contingency is not closely related to the question of the relative adequacy of the foreign-holder's liquidity. In fact, the demand may be less likely to be made by a foreign central bank which is under pressure and which is actively drawing upon its reserves than by one whose external payments are balanced and whose liquidity resources are absolutely and relatively high.

VII. SUMMARY AND CONCLUSIONS

The subject examined in this paper is the nature and determinants of external monetary liquidity, with special reference to the situation of the financially advanced countries. In this examination it has been necessary to look closely at such questions as: what liquidity is for the individual country and how it is functionally defined; the nature of the demand function behind the "requirements" for liquidity; the sources of supply; the meaning of "adequacy" and the measures of it in a theoretical sense; the statistical record of the past ten years, for each of the Group of Ten countries, with reference to these measures of adequacy; and the dynamic prospects for adequate liquidity in the future. Short notes are also included on the composition of liquidity, as distinct from its total amount.

Approaching the subject always from the standpoint of the individual country, which is the relevant and functioning unit to be considered in problems of monetary policy, we defined external liquidity as such resources as are readily available to its monetary authority for the purpose of financing temporary deficits in its balance of payments and defending the stability of its rate of exchange. As defined and interpreted herein, a country's liquidity constitutes a total which is both greater in amount and more flexible than its owned monetary reserves, owing to the (sometimes substantial) credit availabilities.

The assumption has been popularized by recent writers that requirements for liquidity are described by a function stating a constant percentage ratio of (owned) reserves to imports. Since the functional purpose of liquidity is to finance temporary imbalances in the country's external payments, it proves to be less relevant to relate liquidity to the value of imports than to the nation's net external imbalances. Likewise, the notion that liquidity requirements are tied in a fixed (and even rising) ratio to the country's total international transactions also appears questionable. These relationships and the theoretical conclusions about them were illustrated by the statistical experience of the advanced countries in the period 1953-1962, a record which does not appear to lend support to the customary hypothesis about the evolution of the requirements function. It was also observed that both the supply of liquidity and its annual growth have heretofore sometimes been underestimated.

On the basis of the analysis and of the statistical evidence, this paper did not find that the hypothesis of a progressively deteriorating adequacy of liquidity for the major advanced countries had been firmly substantiated. It is possible that new evidence may be forthcoming later to corroborate that thesis. If so, the means for dealing with such a situation are already considerable and are capable of expansion. International cooperation in the monetary sphere—which sometimes operates to reduce liquidity requirements of a deficit country (e.g., through offers of advanced debt repayment by a surplus country) and sometimes to increase liquidity supply (e.g., I.M.F. credits)—shows no lack of inventiveness. The present paper does not examine any of the varied proposals for reform of the international monetary system.[42]

[42] The author hopes he has been correct also in assuming that what the liquidity-adequacy debate is about is, as our definition specifies, the means for financing relatively *temporary* imbalances of payments. If anyone should be seeking a means whereby the country's owned-reserve assets and its additional facilities available *on credit* could somehow be supplemented by non-repayable grants, so as to permit the incurring of permanent payments deficits without the "constraints" of financial policy, that would be a different quest altogether. It would be more pertinent to less-developed than to advanced countries.

STATISTICAL ANNEX

I. EXTERNAL LIQUIDITY OF MONETARY AUTHORITY IN RELATION TO IMPORTS AND TO NET OVERALL EXTERNAL BALANCE, 1953-1963. TABLES AND CHARTS BY COUNTRY.

TABLE I-a, BELGIUM-LUXEMBOURG

External Liquidity of Monetary Authority, in Relation to Imports and to Net Overall External Balance, 1953-1963
($ millions)

	1953	1954	1955	1956	1957	1958	1959	1960	1961	1962	1963
1. Official Reserves	1,088	1,042	1,147	1,163	1,142	1,497	1,222	1,422	1,657	1,622	1,802
Gold	776	778	928	925	915	1,270	1,134	1,170	1,248	1,365	1,371
Foreign Exchange	312	264	219	238	227	227	88	252	409	257	431
2. IMF Total-Tranche Position	281	281	281	281	231	281	422	422	414	469	475
3. Total (official) External Liquidity (1 + 2)	1,369	1,323	1,428	1,444	1,373	1,778	1,644	1,844	2,151	2,091	2,277
4. Value of Imports (cif)	2,413	2,535	2,830	3,272	3,432	3,129	3,442	3,957	4,219	4,555	5,098
5. Liquidity Ratio A. (3:4) = Total External Liquidity / Imports	.57	.52	.50	.44	.40	.57	.48	.47	.51	.46	.45
6. Net Overall External Balance	22	2	122	50	32	392	−188	166	74	—	—
7. Liquidity Ratio B. (3:6) = Total External Liquidity / Net Overall External Balance	62.2	661.5	11.7	28.9	42.9	4.5	*8.7	11.1	29.1	—	—

Notes and Sources: See summary tables.

44

TABLE I-b, CANADA

External Liquidity of Monetary Authority, in Relation to Imports and to Net Overall External Balance, 1953-1963
($ millions)

	1953	1954	1955	1956	1957	1958	1959	1960	1961	1962	1963
1. Official Reserves	1,827	1,954	1,910	1,944	1,836	1,948	1,876	1,836	2,064	2,546	2,603
Gold	986	1,073	1,134	1,103	1,100	1,078	960	885	946	708	817
Foreign Exchange	841	882	776	841	736	870	917	951	1,118	1,838	1,786
2. IMF Total-Tranche Position	375	375	375	390	390	390	703	703	762	412	492
3. Total (official) External Liquidity (1 + 2)	2,202	2,329	2,285	2,334	2,226	2,338	2,579	2,539	2,826	2,958	3,095
4. Value of Imports (cif)	4,697	4,433	5,020	6,110	6,188	5,638	6,242	6,150	6,193	6,367	6,618
5. Liquidity Ratio A. (3:4) = Total External Liquidity / Imports	.47	.53	.46	.38	.36	.41	.41	.41	.46	.46	.47
6. Net Overall External Balance	78	182	−218	293	211	64	111	−46	142	84	—
7. Liquidity Ratio B. (3:6) = Total External Liquidity / Net Overall External Balance	28.2	12.8	*10.5	8.0	10.5	36.5	23.2	*55.2	19.9	35.2	—

Notes and Sources: See summary tables.

45

TABLE I-c, FRANCE

External Liquidity of Monetary Authority, in Relation to Imports and to Net Overall External Balance, 1953-1963
($ millions)

	1953	1954	1955	1956	1957	1958	1959	1960	1961	1962	1963
1. Official Reserves	829	1,261	1,912	1,180	645	1,050	1,720	2,070	2,939	3,610	4,457
Gold	617	708	942	924	581	750	1,290	1,641	2,121	2,587	3,175
Foreign Exchange	212	553	970	256	64	300	430	429	818	1,023	1,282
2. IMF Total-Tranche Position	[525]	528	588	656	394	263	803	989	1,214	1,226	1,238
3. Total (official) External Liquidity (1 + 2)	1,354	1,789	2,500	1,836	1,039	1,313	2,523	3,059	4,153	4,836	5,695
4. Value of Imports (cif)	3,942	4,221	4,739	5,558	6,175	5,609	5,088	6,281	6,679	7,517	8,727
5. Liquidity Ratio A. (3:4) = Total External Liquidity / Imports	.34	.42	.53	.33	.17	.23	.50	.49	.62	.64	.65
6. Net Overall External Balance	168	620	745	−718	−1,305	25	1,590	485	957	608	—
7. Liquidity Ratio B. (3:6) = Total External Liquidity / Net Overall External Balance	8.1	2.9	3.4	*2.6	*0.8	52.5	1.6	6.3	4.3	8.0	—

Notes and Sources: See summary tables.

TABLE I-d, GERMANY

External Liquidity of Monetary Authority, in Relation to Imports and to Net Overall External Balance, 1953-1963
($ millions)

	1953	1954	1955	1956	1957	1958	1959	1960	1961	1962	1963
1. Official Reserves	1,736	2,496	2,934	4,119	5,114	5,732	4,533	6,737	6,542	6,447	7,098
Gold	325	626	920	1,494	2,541	2,639	2,637	2,971	3,664	3,679	3,843
Foreign Exchange	1,411	1,870	2,014	2,625	2,573	3,093	1,896	3,766	2,878	2,768	3,255
2. IMF Total-Tranche Position	367	413	413	413	413	477	1,056	1,096	1,425	1,305	1,340
3. Total (official) External Liquidity (1 + 2)	2,103	2,903	3,347	4,532	5,527	6,209	5,589	7,833	7,967	7,752	8,438
4. Value of Imports (cif)	3,771	4,571	5,793	6,617	7,542	7,576	8,482	10,107	10,948	12,289	13,023
5. Liquidity Ratio A. (3:4) = Total External Liquidity / Imports	.56	.64	.58	.68	.73	.82	.66	.78	.73	.63	.65
6. Net Overall External Balance	772	771	484	1,024	1,121	933	−908	1,684	163	−183	—
7. Liquidity Ratio B. (3:6) = Total External Liquidity / Net Overall External Balance	2.7	3.8	6.9	4.4	4.9	6.7	*6.2	4.7	48.9	*42.4	—

Notes and Sources: See summary tables.

47

TABLE I-e, ITALY

External Liquidity of Monetary Authority, in Relation to Imports and to Net Overall External Balance, 1953-1963
($ millions)

	1953	1954	1955	1956	1957	1958	1959	1960	1961	1962	1963
1. Official Reserves	768	927	1,167	1,236	1,354	2,082	2,953	3,079	3,419	3,441	3,057
Gold	346	346	352	338	452	1,086	1,749	2,203	2,225	2,243	2,343
Foreign Exchange	422	581	815	898	903	996	1,204	876	1,194	1,198	714
2. IMF Total-Tranche Position	[180	180	180	180	180	180]	338	338	513	473	496
3. Total (official) External Liquidity (1 + 2)	948	1,107	1,347	1,416	1,534	2,262	3,291	3,417	3,932	3,914	3,553
4. Value of Imports (cif)	2,420	2,439	2,711	3,174	3,674	3,216	3,369	4,725	5,223	6,056	7,539
5. Liquidity Ratio A. (3:4) = Total External Liquidity / Imports	.39	.45	.49	.45	.42	.70	.98	.72	.75	.65	.47
6. Net Overall External Balance	−83	−8	80	35	169	721	804	460	489	−376	—
7. Liquidity Ratio B. (3:6) = Total External Liquidity / Net Overall External Balance	*11.4	*138.3	16.8	40.5	9.1	3.1	4.0	7.4	8.0	*10.4	—

Notes and Sources: See summary tables.

TABLE I-f, JAPAN

External Liquidity of Monetary Authority, in Relation to Imports and to Net Overall External Balance, 1953-1963

($ millions)

	1953	1954	1955	1956	1957	1958	1959	1960	1961	1962	1963
1. Official Reserves	823	738	769	941	524	861	1,322	1,824	1,486	1,842	1,978
Gold	18	21	23	23	23	54	244	247	287	289	—
Foreign Exchange	805	717	746	918	501	807	1,077	1,577	1,199	1,553	—
2. IMF Total-Tranche Position	250	250	312	312	188	312	625	625	680	680	680
3. Total (official) External Liquidity (1 + 2)	1,073	988	1,081	1,253	712	1,173	1,947	2,449	2,166	2,522	2,658
4. Value of Imports (cif)	2,410	2,399	2,471	3,230	4,284	3,033	3,599	4,491	5,811	5,637	6,737
5. Liquidity Ratio A. (3:4) = Total External Liquidity / Imports	.45	.41	.44	.39	.17	.39	.54	.55	.37	.45	.39
6. Net Overall External Balance	−234	−20	257	2	−546	414	390	104	−957	—	—
7. Liquidity Ratio B. (3:6) = Total External Liquidity / Net Overall External Balance	*4.6	*49.4	4.2	626.5	*1.3	2.8	5.0	23.5	*2.3	—	—

Notes and Sources: See summary tables.

TABLE I-g, NETHERLANDS

External Liquidity of Monetary Authority, in Relation to Imports and to Net Overall External Balance, 1953-1963
($ millions)

	1953	1954	1955	1956	1957	1958	1959	1960	1961	1962	1963
1. Official Reserves	1,163	1,209	1,223	1,038	1,009	1,470	1,339	1,742	1,715	1,743	1,889
Gold	737	796	865	844	744	1,050	1,132	1,451	1,581	1,581	1,601
Foreign Exchange	426	413	358	194	265	420	207	291	134	162	298
2. IMF Total-Tranche Position	344	344	344	344	275	344	516	533	655	615	615
3. Total (official) External Liquidity (1 + 2)	1,507	1,553	1,567	1,382	1,284	1,814	1,855	2,275	2,370	2,358	2,514
4. Value of Imports (cif)	2,376	2,858	3,209	3,726	4,106	3,625	3,940	4,531	5,087	5,347	5,968
5. Liquidity Ratio A. (3:4) = Total External Liquidity / Imports	.63	.54	.49	.37	.31	.50	.47	.50	.47	.44	.42
6. Net Overall External Balance	297	120	55	−190	18	540	196	410	−26	−39	—
7. Liquidity Ratio B. (3:6) = Total External Liquidity / Net Overall External Balance	5.1	12.9	28.5	*7.3	71.3	3.4	9.5	5.5	*91.2	*60.4	—

Notes and Sources: See summary tables.

50

TABLE I-h, SWEDEN

External Liquidity of Monetary Authority, in Relation to Imports and to Net Overall External Balance, 1953-1963
($ millions)

	1953	1954	1955	1956	1957	1958	1959	1960	1961	1962	1963
1. Official Reserves	534	518	497	510	476	491	440	490	673	754	706
Gold	219	265	276	266	219	204	190	170	180	181	182
Foreign Exchange	315	253	221	244	257	287	249	320	492	573	524
2. IMF Total-Tranche Position	125	125	125	125	125	125	188	188	213	198	203
3. Total (official) External Liquidity (1 + 2)	659	643	622	635	601	616	628	678	886	952	909
4. Value of Imports (cif)	1,579	1,776	1,997	2,209	2,428	2,367	2,413	2,899	2,927	3,121	3,389
5. Liquidity Ratio A. (3:4) = Total External Liquidity / Imports	.42	.36	.31	.28	.25	.26	.26	.23	.30	.31	.27
6. Net Overall External Balance	65	13	20	52	24	39	25	−28	200	—	—
7. Liquidity Ratio B. (3:6) = Total External Liquidity / Net Overall External Balance	10.1	49.5	31.1	12.2	25.0	15.8	25.1	*24.2	4.4	—	—

Notes and Sources: See summary tables.

TABLE I-i, SWITZERLAND

External Liquidity of Monetary Authority, in Relation to Imports and to Net Overall External Balance, 1953-1963
($ millions)

	1953	1954	1955	1956	1957	1958	1959	1960	1961	1962	1963
1. Official Reserves	1,768	1,837	1,847	1,882	1,898	2,063	2,063	2,324	2,759	2,872	3,074
Gold	1,458	1,513	1,597	1,664	1,706	1,925	1,934	2,185	2,560	2,667	2,820
Foreign Exchange	310	324	250	218	192	138	129	139	199	204	254
2. IMF Total-Tranche Position	non member	—	—	—	—	—	—	—	—	—	—
3. Total (official) External Liquidity (1+2)	1,768	1,837	1,847	1,882	1,898	2,063	2,063	2,324	2,759	2,872	3,074
4. Value of Imports (cif)	1,176	1,300	1,489	1,766	1,964	1,706	1,923	2,243	2,707	3,020	3,253
5. Liquidity Ratio A. (3:4) = Total External Liquidity / Imports	1.50	1.41	1.24	1.07	.97	1.21	1.07	1.04	1.02	.95	1.06
6. Net Overall External Balance	109	148	64	138	88	302	7	255	438	—	—
7. Liquidity Ratio B. (3:6) = Total External Liquidity / Net Overall External Balance	16.2	12.4	28.9	13.6	21.6	6.8	294.7	9.1	6.3	—	—

Notes and Sources: See summary tables.

TABLE I-j, UNITED KINGDOM

External Liquidity of Monetary Authority, in Relation to Imports and to Net Overall External Balance, 1953-1963
($ millions)

	1953	1954	1955	1956	1957	1958	1959	1960	1961	1962	1963
1. Official Reserves	2,546	2,798	2,156	2,276	2,374	3,105	2,750	3,239	3,324	2,809	2,657
Gold	2,263	2,530	2,012	1,773	1,555	2,807	2,514	2,801	2,267	2,581	2,484
Foreign Exchange	283	268	144	503	819	298	236	438	1,057	228	173
2. IMF Total-Tranche Position	1,424	1,536	1,536	971	966	982	2,015	2,438	1,392	2,452	2,439
3. Total (official) External Liquidity (1 + 2)	3,970	4,334	3,692	3,247	3,340	4,087	4,765	5,677	4,716	5,261	5,096
4. Value of Imports (cif)	9,314	9,405	10,809	10,812	11,322	10,493	11,153	12,714	12,308	12,563	13,497
5. Liquidity Ratio A. (3:4) = Total External Liquidity / Imports	.43	.46	.34	.30	.30	.39	.43	.45	.38	.42	.38
6. Net Overall External Balance	−47	−179	−485	117	521	449	2	14	−872	490	—
7. Liquidity Ratio B. (3:6) = Total External Liquidity / Net Overall External Balance	*84.5	*24.2	*7.6	27.8	6.4	9.1	2382.5	405.5	*12.7	10.7	—

Notes and Sources: See summary tables.

TABLE I-k, UNITED STATES

External Liquidity of Monetary Authority, in Relation to Imports and to Net Overall External Balance, 1953-1963
($ millions)

	1953	1954	1955	1956	1957	1958	1959	1960	1961	1962	1963
1. Official Reserves	22,091	21,793	21,753	22,058	22,857	20,582	19,507	17,804	17,063	16,156	15,808
Gold	22,091	21,793	21,753	22,058	22,857	20,582	19,507	17,804	16,947	16,057	15,596
Foreign Exchange	—	—	—	—	—	—	—	—	116	99	212
2. IMF Total-Tranche Position	4,117	3,935	3,794	4,358	4,725	4,708	6,122	5,680	5,815	5,189	5,160
3. Total (official) External Liquidity (1 + 2)	26,208	25,728	25,547	26,416	27,582	25,290	25,629	23,484	22,878	21,346	20,968
3-a External Liquidity (line 3) incl. Bilateral-Credit Facilities											23,018[1]
4. Value of Imports (cif)	11,846	11,140	12,489	13,987	14,620	14,619	17,013	16,508	16,069	17,764	18,600
5. Liquidity Ratio A. (3:4) = Total External Liquidity / Imports	2.21	2.31	2.05	1.89	1.89	1.73	1.51	1.42	1.42	1.19	1.13
6. Net Overall External Balance	-2,308	-1,062	-983	-549	776	-3,178	-3,686	-2,930	-1,339	-1,909	—
7. Liquidity Ratio B. (3:6) = Total External Liquidity / Net Overall External Balance	*11.4	*24.2	*26.0	*48.1	35.5	*8.0	*7.0	*8.0	*17.1	*11.2	—

Notes and Sources: See summary tables.

[1] Line 3-a equals line 3 plus $2,050 billion in bilateral-credit (swap) facilities. It would be more consistent with our general definition to deduct from the latter figure the relatively small amount of such facilities utilized, but this breakdown is not presently available.

54

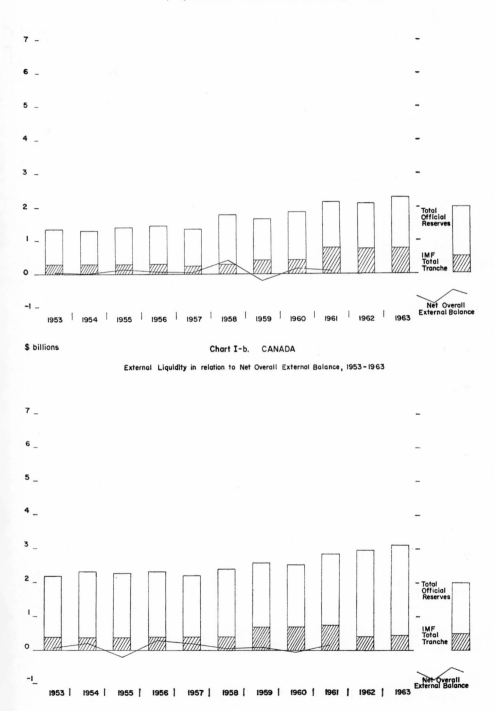

$ billions   Chart I-a. BELGIUM - LUXEMBOURG

External Liquidity in relation to Net Overall External Balance, 1953-1963

Total Official Reserves

IMF Total Tranche

Net Overall External Balance

1953 1954 1955 1956 1957 1958 1959 1960 1961 1962 1963

$ billions   Chart I-b. CANADA

External Liquidity in relation to Net Overall External Balance, 1953-1963

Total Official Reserves

IMF Total Tranche

Net Overall External Balance

1953 1954 1955 1956 1957 1958 1959 1960 1961 1962 1963

55

$ billions   Chart I-c.   FRANCE

External Liquidity in relation to Net Overall External Balance, 1953-1963

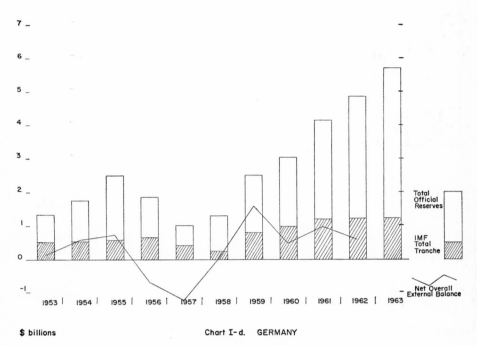

$ billions   Chart I-d.   GERMANY

External   Liquidity in relation to Net Overall External Balance, 1953-1963

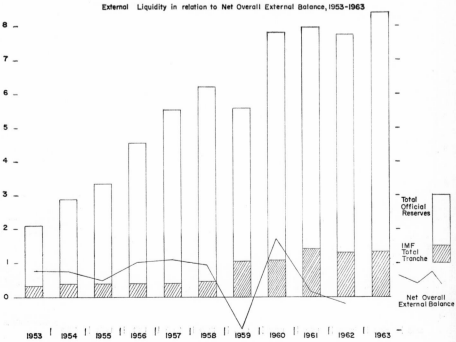

$ billions   Chart I-e.   ITALY

External Liquidity in relation to Net Overall External Balance, 1953-1963

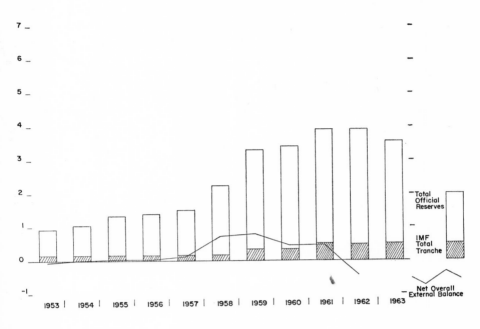

$ billions   Chart I-f.   JAPAN

External Liquidity in relation to Net Overall External Balance, 1953-1963

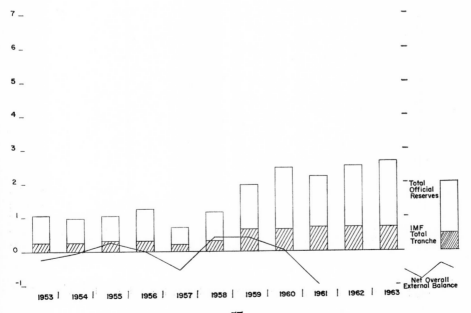

$ billions   Chart I-g.   NETHERLANDS

External Liquidity in relation to Net Overall External Balance, 1953-1963

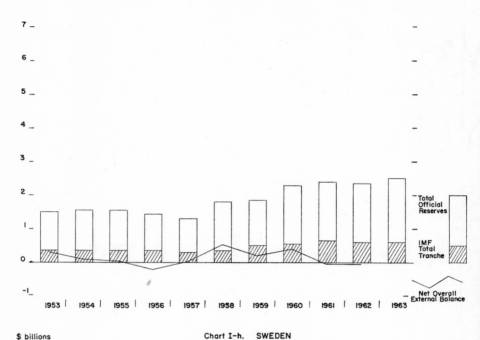

$ billions   Chart I-h.   SWEDEN

External Liquidity in relation to Net Overall External Balance, 1953-1963

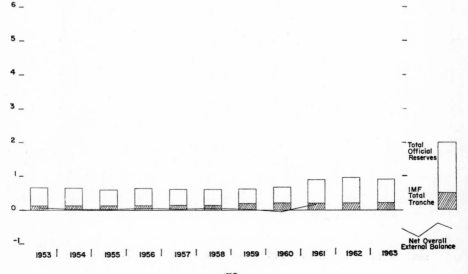

$ billions
Chart I-i   SWITZERLAND

External Liquidity in relation to Net Overall External Balance, 1953-1963

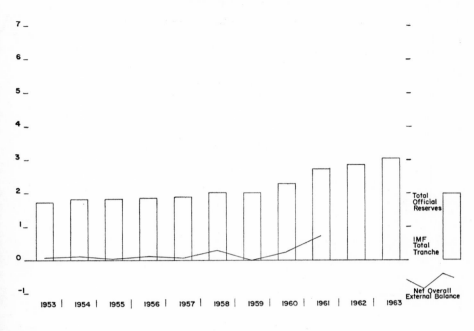

$ billions
Chart I-j   UNITED KINGDOM

External Liquidity in relation to Net Overall External Balance, 1953-1963

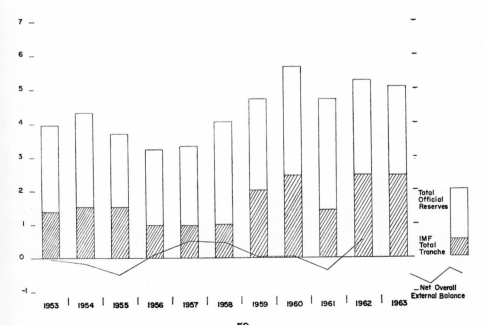

External Liquidity in relation to Net Overall External Balance, 1953-1963

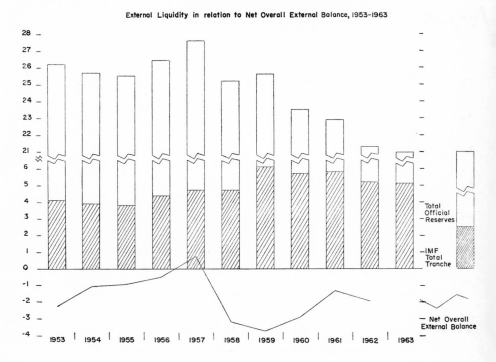

II. EXTERNAL LIQUIDITY, VALUE OF IMPORTS, NET OVERALL EXTERNAL BALANCES, AND LIQUIDITY RATIOS. BY COUNTRY AND FOR THE GROUP OF COUNTRIES.

Table II-a, Total (official) External Liquidity of Group of Ten Countries, 1953-1963
[Gold and Foreign Exchange Reserves, plus Gross IMF Position (Total-Tranche Position)]
(end of year, in $ millions)

	1953	1954	1955	1956	1957	1958	1959	1960	1961	1962	1963
Belgium-Luxembourg											
1. Official-Reserves (total)	1,088	1,042	1,147	1,163	1,142	1,497	1,222	1,422	1,657	1,622	1,802
2. IMF Total-Tranche Position	281	281	281	281	231	281	422	422	494	469	475
3. Total (official) External Liquidity (1 + 2)	1,369	1,323	1,428	1,444	1,373	1,778	1,644	1,844	2,151	2,091	2,277
Canada											
1. Official-Reserves (total)	1,827	1,954	1,910	1,944	1,836	1,948	1,876	1,836	2,064	2,546	2,603
2. IMF Total-Tranche Position	375	375	375	390	390	390	703	703	762	412	492
3. Total (official) External Liquidity (1 + 2)	2,202	2,329	2,285	2,334	2,226	2,338	2,579	2,539	2,826	2,958	3,095
France											
1. Official-Reserves (total)	829	1,261	1,912	1,180	645	1,050	1,720	2,070	2,939	3,610	4,457
2. IMF Total-Tranche Position	¹525	528	588	656	394	263	803	989	1,214	1,226	1,238
3. Total (official) External Liquidity (1 + 2)	1,354	1,789	2,500	1,836	1,039	1,313	2,523	3,059	4,153	4,836	5,695
Germany											
1. Official-Reserves (total)	1,736	2,496	2,934	4,119	5,114	5,732	4,533	6,737	6,542	6,447	7,098
2. IMF Total-Tranche Position	367	413	413	413	413	477	1,056	1,096	1,425	1,305	1,340
3. Total (official) External Liquidity (1 + 2)	2,103	2,909	3,347	4,532	5,527	6,209	5,589	7,833	7,967	7,752	8,438
Italy											
1. Official-Reserves (total)	768	927	1,167	1,236	1,354	2,082	2,953	3,079	3,419	3,441	3,057
2. IMF Total-Tranche Position	²[180	180	180	180	180	180]	338	338	513	473	496
3. Total (official) External Liquidity (1 + 2)	948	1,107	1,347	1,416	1,534	2,262	3,291	3,417	3,932	3,914	3,553
Japan											
1. Official-Reserves (total)	823	738	769	941	524	861	1,322	1,824	1,486	1,842	1,978
2. IMF Total-Tranche Position	250	250	312	312	188	312	625	625	680	680	680
3. Total (official) External Liquidity (1 + 2)	1,073	988	1,081	1,253	712	1,173	1,947	2,449	2,166	2,522	2,658
Netherlands											
1. Official-Reserves (total)	1,163	1,209	1,223	1,038	1,009	1,470	1,339	1,742	1,715	1,743	1,899
2. IMF Total-Tranche Position	344	344	344	344	275	344	516	533	655	615	615
3. Total (official) External Liquidity (1 + 2)	1,507	1,553	1,567	1,382	1,284	1,814	1,855	2,275	2,370	2,358	2,514

	1953	1954	1955	1956	1957	1958	1959	1960	1961	1962	1963
Sweden											
1. Official-Reserves (total)	534	518	497	510	476	491	440	490	673	754	706
2. IMF Total-Tranche Position	125	125	125	125	125	125	188	188	213	198	203
3. Total (official) External Liquidity (1 + 2)	659	643	622	635	601	616	628	678	886	952	909
Switzerland											
1. Official-Reserves (total)	1,768	1,837	1,847	1,882	1,898	2,063	2,063	2,324	2,759	2,872	3,074
2. non-member	—	—	—	—	—	—	—	—	—	—	—
3. Total (official) External Liquidity (1 + 2)	1,768	1,837	1,847	1,882	1,898	2,063	2,063	2,324	2,759	2,872	3,074
United Kingdom											
1. Official-Reserves (total)	2,546	2,798	2,156	2,276	2,374	3,105	2,750	3,239	3,324	2,809	2,657
2. IMF Total-Tranche Position	1,424	1,536	1,536	971	966	982	2,015	2,438	1,392	2,452	2,439
3. Total (official) External Liquidity (1 + 2)	3,970	4,334	3,692	3,247	3,340	4,087	4,765	5,677	4,716	5,261	5,096
United States											
1. Official-Reserves (total)	22,091	21,793	21,753	22,058	22,857	20,582	19,507	17,804	17,063	16,156	15,808
2. IMF Total-Tranche Position	4,117	3,935	3,794	4,358	4,725	4,708	6,122	5,680	5,815	5,189	5,160
3. Total (official) External Liquidity (1 + 2)	26,208	25,728	25,547	26,416	27,582	25,290	25,629	23,484	22,878	21,346	20,968

The Group of Ten countries consist of the ten I.M.F. members (plus Switzerland) listed in the table. These are the advanced countries which "have undertaken, in accordance with the General Arrangements to Borrow adopted by the Fund in 1962, to lend to the Fund specified amounts of their currencies if needed to forestall or cope with an impairment of the international monetary system." (I.M.F., *International Financial Statistics*, December 1963, p. 8). Switzerland, although not a member of the Fund, is associated closely with the Group of Ten.

In Table II-a and the country tables, the figures on "official reserves" are the official holdings of the monetary authority in gold and foreign exchange. The I.M.F. "Total-Tranche Position" as given in the tables is defined by the Fund as "The sum of the Gold Tranche and Credit Tranche Position, i.e., twice the member's quota minus the Fund's holdings of the member's currency. In earlier issues of IFS the Total Tranche Position was called the Gross I.M.F. position." (*International Financial Statistics*, December 1963, p. 7).

SOURCES:

I.M.F., *International Financial Statistics*, January 1964, pages 16 to 19 and country pages
April 1964, pages 16 to 19 and country pages

NOTES:

1 France's 1953 quota
2 Italy's quota from 1953 to 1958

63

Table II-b, Value of Imports (annual, cif) 1953-1963

($ millions)

	1953	1954	1955	1956	1957	1958	1959	1960	1961	1962	1963
Belgium-Luxembourg	2,413	2,535	2,830	3,272	3,432	3,129	3,442	3,957	4,219	4,555	5,098
Canada	4,697	4,433	5,020	6,110	6,188	5,638	6,242	6,150	6,193	6,367	6,618
France	3,942	4,221	4,739	5,558	6,175	5,609	5,088	6,281	6,679	7,517	8,727
Germany	3,771	4,571	5,793	6,617	7,542	7,576	8,482	10,107	10,948	12,289	13,023
Italy	2,420	2,439	2,711	3,174	3,674	3,216	3,369	4,725	5,223	6,056	7,539
Japan	2,410	2,399	2,471	3,230	4,284	3,033	3,599	4,491	5,811	5,637	6,737
Netherlands	2,376	2,858	3,209	3,726	4,106	3,625	3,940	4,531	5,087	5,347	5,968
Sweden	1,579	1,776	1,997	2,209	2,428	2,367	2,413	2,899	2,927	3,121	3,389
Switzerland	1,176	1,300	1,489	1,766	1,964	1,706	1,923	2,243	2,707	3,020	3,253
Total 9 countries	24,784	26,532	30,259	35,662	39,793	35,899	38,498	45,384	49,796	53,909	60,352
United Kingdom	9,314	9,405	10,809	10,812	11,322	10,493	11,153	12,714	12,308	12,563	13,497
United States	11,846	11,140	12,489	13,987	14,620	14,319	17,013	16,508	16,069	17,764	18,600
Total 11 countries	45,944	47,077	53,557	60,461	65,735	61,011	66,664	74,606	78,173	84,236	92,449

Sources: I.M.F., *International Financial Statistics*, January 1964, page 35
April 1964, page 35

Table II-c
Net Overall External Balance of International Payments, 1953-1962
($ millions)

	1953	1954	1955	1956	1957	1958	1959	1960	1961	1962
Belgium-Luxembourg	22	2	122	50	32	392	−188	166	74	—
Canada	78	182	−218	293	211	64	111	−46	142	84
France	168	620	745	−718	−1,305	25	1,590	485	957	608
Germany	772	771	484	1,024	1,121	933	−908	1,684	163	−183
Italy	−83	−8	80	35	169	721	804	460	489	−376
Japan	−234	−20	257	2	−546	414	390	104	−957	—
Netherlands	297	120	55	−190	18	540	196	410	−26	−39
Sweden	65	13	20	52	24	39	25	−28	200	—
Switzerland	109	148	64	138	88	302	7	255	438	—
United Kingdom	−47	−179	−485	117	521	449	2	14	−372	490
United States	−2,308	−1,062	−983	−549	776	−3,178	−3,686	−2,930	−1,339	−1,909

Source: The above data were made available by the Secretariat of the O.E.C.D. The figures given are those for "overall balance," as derived by the O.E.C.D. from balance-of-payment data submitted by national authorities and adjusted to achieve the greatest international comparability. Data for Japan on the basis presented here are regarded as more provisional than for other countries. For 1962, the figures for some countries are not available, and those given are preliminary.

Table II-d, Liquidity Ratios:

Relation of External Liquidity (A) to Imports and (B) to Net Overall External Balance, 1953-1963

	1953	1954	1955	1956	1957	1958	1959	1960	1961	1962	1963
Belgium-Luxembourg											
(A) Liquidity: Imports	.57	.52	.50	.44	.40	.57	.48	.47	.51	.46	.45
(B) Liquidity: Net Overall External Balance	62.2	661.5	11.7	28.9	42.9	4.5	*8.7	11.1	29.1	—	—
Canada											
(A) Liquidity: Imports	.47	.53	.46	.38	.36	.41	.41	.41	.46	.46	.47
(B) Liquidity: Net Overall External Balance	28.2	12.8	*10.5	8.0	10.5	36.5	23.2	*55.2	19.9	35.2	—
France											
(A) Liquidity: Imports	.34	.42	.53	.33	.17	.23	.50	.49	.62	.64	.65
(B) Liquidity: Net Overall External Balance	8.1	2.9	3.4	*2.6	*0.8	52.5	1.6	6.3	4.3	8.0	—
Germany											
(A) Liquidity: Imports	.56	.64	.58	.68	.73	.82	.66	.78	.73	.63	.65
(B) Liquidity: Net Overall External Balance	2.7	3.8	6.9	4.4	4.9	6.7	*6.2	4.7	48.9	*42.4	—
Italy											
(A) Liquidity: Imports	.39	.45	.49	.45	.42	.70	.98	.72	.75	.65	.47
(B) Liquidity: Net Overall External Balance	*11.4	*138.3	16.8	40.5	9.1	3.1	4.0	7.4	8.0	*10.4	—
Japan											
(A) Liquidity: Imports	.45	.41	.44	.39	.17	.39	.54	.55	.37	.45	.39
(B) Liquidity: Net Overall External Balance	*4.6	*49.4	4.2	626.5	*1.3	2.8	5.0	23.5	*2.3	—	—
Netherlands											
(A) Liquidity: Imports	.63	.54	.49	.37	.31	.50	.47	.50	.47	.44	.42
(B) Liquidity: Net Overall External Balance	5.1	12.9	28.5	*7.3	71.3	3.4	9.5	5.5	*91.2	*60.4	—
Sweden											
(A) Liquidity: Imports	.42	.36	.31	.28	.25	.26	.26	.23	.30	.31	.27
(B) Liquidity: Net Overall External Balance	10.1	49.5	31.1	12.2	25.0	15.8	25.1	*24.2	4.4	—	—
Switzerland											
(A) Liquidity: Imports	1.50	1.41	1.24	1.07	.97	1.21	1.07	1.04	1.02	.95	1.06
(B) Liquidity: Net Overall External Balance	16.2	12.4	28.9	13.6	21.6	6.8	294.7	9.1	6.3	—	—
United Kingdom											
(A) Liquidity: Imports	.43	.46	.34	.30	.30	.39	.43	.45	.38	.42	.38
(B) Liquidity: Net Overall External Balance	*84.5	*24.2	*7.6	27.8	6.4	9.1	2382.5	405.5	*12.7	10.7	—
United States											
(A) Liquidity: Imports	2.21	2.31	2.05	1.89	1.89	1.73	1.51	1.42	1.42	1.19	1.13
(B) Liquidity: Net Overall External Balance	*11.4	*24.2	*26.0	*48.1	35.5	*8.0	*7.0	*8.0	*17.1	*11.2	—

Notes and Sources: See summary tables II a, b, and c.   * An asterisk denotes that the net overall external balance in the

PUBLICATIONS OF THE
INTERNATIONAL FINANCE SECTION

The International Finance Section publishes at irregular intervals papers in three series: ESSAYS IN INTERNATIONAL FINANCE, PRINCETON STUDIES IN INTERNATIONAL FINANCE, and SPECIAL PAPERS IN INTERNATIONAL ECONOMICS. All three of these may be ordered directly from the Section.

Single copies of the ESSAYS are distributed without charge to all interested persons, both here and abroad. Additional copies of any one issue may be obtained from the Section at a charge of $0.25 a copy, payable in advance. This charge may be waived to foreign institutions of education or research.

For the STUDIES and SPECIAL PAPERS there will be a charge of $1.00 a copy. This charge will be waived on copies distributed to college and university libraries here and abroad. In addition, the charge is sometimes waived on single copies requested by persons residing abroad who find it difficult to make remittance.

For the convenience of our British customers, arrangements have been made for retail distribution of the STUDIES and SPECIAL PAPERS through the Economists' Bookshop, Portugal Street, London, W.C. 2, and Blackwells, Broad Street, Oxford. These booksellers will usually have our publications in stock.

A mailing list is maintained for the distribution of ESSAYS as they are issued and of announcements of new issues in the series of STUDIES and SPECIAL PAPERS. Requests for inclusion in this list will be honored, except that students will not be placed on the permanent mailing list, because waste results from frequent changes of addresses.

The following is a complete list of the publications of the International Finance Section. The issues of the three series that are still available from the Section are marked by asterisks. Those marked by daggers are out of stock at the International Finance Section but may be obtained in xerographic reproductions (that is, looking like the originals) from University Microfilms, Inc., 313 N. First Street, Ann Arbor, Michigan, 48107. (Most of the issues are priced at $2.50.)

ESSAYS IN INTERNATIONAL FINANCE

† No. 1. Friedrich A. Lutz, International Monetary Mechanisms: The Keynes and White Proposals. (July 1943)
†   2. Frank D. Graham, Fundamentals of International Monetary Policy. (Autumn 1943)

†   3. Richard A. Lester, International Aspects of Wartime Monetary Experience. (Aug. 1944)

†   4. Ragnar Nurkse, Conditions of International Monetary Equilibrium. (Spring 1945)

†   5. Howard S. Ellis, Bilateralism and the Future of International Trade. (Summer 1945)

†   6. Arthur I. Bloomfield, The British Balance-of-Payments Problem. (Autumn 1945)

†   7. Frank A. Southard, Jr., Some European Currency and Exchange Experiences. (Summer 1946)

†   8. Miroslav A. Kriz, Postwar International Lending. (Spring 1947)

†   9. Friedrich A. Lutz, The Marshall Plan and European Economic Policy. (Spring 1948)

† 10. Frank D. Graham, The Cause and Cure of "Dollar Shortage." (Jan. 1949)

† 11. Horst Mendershausen, Dollar Shortage and Oil Surplus in 1949-1950. (Nov. 1950)

† 12. Sir Arthur Salter, Foreign Investment. (Feb. 1951)

† 13. Sir Roy Harrod, The Pound Sterling. (Feb. 1952)

† 14. S. Herbert Frankel, Some Conceptual Aspects of International Economic Development of Underdeveloped Territories. (May 1952)

† 15. Miroslav A. Kriz, The Price of Gold. (July 1952)

† 16. William Diebold, Jr., The End of the I.T.O. (Oct. 1952)

† 17. Sir Douglas Copland, Problems of the Sterling Area: With Special Reference to Australia. (Sept. 1953)

† 18. Raymond F. Mikesell, The Emerging Pattern of International Payments. (April 1954)

† 19. D. Gale Johnson, Agricultural Price Policy and International Trade. (June 1954)

† 20. Ida Greaves, "The Colonial Sterling Balances." (Sept. 1954)

† 21. Raymond Vernon, America's Foreign Trade Policy and the GATT. (Oct. 1954)

† 22. Roger Auboin, The Bank for International Settlements, 1930-1955. (May 1955)

† 23. Wytze Gorter, United States Merchant Marine Policies: Some International Implications. (June 1955)

† 24. Thomas C. Schelling, International Cost-Sharing Arrangements. (Sept. 1955)

† 25. James E. Meade, The Belgium-Luxembourg Economic Union, 1921-1939. (March 1956)

† 26. Samuel I. Katz, Two Approaches to the Exchange-Rate Problem: The United Kingdom and Canada. (Aug. 1956)

† 27. A. R. Conan, The Changing Pattern of International Investment in Selected Sterling Countries. (Dec. 1956)

† 28. Fred H. Klopstock, The International Status of the Dollar. (May 1957)

† 29. Raymond Vernon, Trade Policy in Crisis. (March 1958)

† 30. Sir Roy Harrod, The Pound Sterling, 1951-1958. (Aug. 1958)

† 31. Randall Hinshaw, Toward European Convertibility. (Nov. 1958)

† 32. Francis H. Schott, The Evolution of Latin American Exchange-Rate Policies since World War II. (Jan. 1959)

† 33. Alec Cairncross, The International Bank for Reconstruction and Development. (March 1959)

SPECIAL PAPERS IN INTERNATIONAL ECONOMICS

No. 1. Gottfried Haberler, A Survey of International Trade Theory. (Revised edition, July 1961)

†   2. Oskar Morgenstern, The Validity of International Gold Movement Statistics. (Nov. 1955)

❋   3. Fritz Machlup, Plans for Reform of the International Monetary System. (Revised edition, March 1964)

†   4. Egon Sohmen, International Monetary Problems and the Foreign Exchanges. (April 1963)

❋   5. Walther Lederer, The Balance on Foreign Transactions: Problems of Definition and Measurement. (Sept. 1963)